LEADING WITH EMOTIONAL INTELLIGENCE

A GUIDE FOR BOARD DIRECTORS

I would like to express my heartfelt gratitude to my family for their unwavering support throughout the incredible journey of writing this book. Your love, encouragement, and understanding have been my pillars of strength and inspiration. Your belief in me is deeply appreciated. Thank you for being my rock, my sounding board, and my constant source of encouragement. This book would not have been possible without your unwavering support, and for that, I am eternally grateful.

LEADING WITH EMOTIONAL INTELLIGENCE

INTELLIGENCE

A GUIDE FOR BOARD DIRECTORS

Sanela Osmic BBus MIB GAICD

ETHICAL
GOVERNANCE

Disclaimer

Please note that the information presented in this material is for educational purposes only and is not intended to provide legal or any other professional advice. The content is meant to be informative and should not be used as a substitute for professional legal or other advice. The use of this material is at your own risk, and Ethical Governance Pty Ltd does not accept any responsibility or liability for any errors or omissions in the information provided. It is always advisable to seek the advice of a qualified professional before making any decisions based on the information presented in this material.

Publisher: Ethical Governance Pty Ltd

Title: Leading With Emotional Intelligence: A Guide for Board Directors

Cover design: cebooker on Fiverr

ISBN: 978-0-6459532-1-3

Table of Contents

ABOUT THE AUTHOR

Sanela Osmic GAICD is the Founder and Managing Director of Ethical Governance. Through acquiring almost 20 years of experience in governance and working with boards in various capacities, Sanela has helped organizations build effective boards, enhance ethical governance practices, and maximize their impact.

Her professional career has spanned multiple industries including finance, professional services, disability, government, and education. Sanela has a talent for distilling complex governance issues into clear, actionable recommendations that drive results. She is known for her ability to navigate difficult situations with grace and diplomacy and has a reputation for being an excellent listener and collaborator. Sanela holds a double degree in Economics and International Trade, and a Master of International Business.

With a proven track record of success and a strong passion for ethical governance, Sanela is the ideal partner to help your organization navigate the complex world of governance and drive success.

PURPOSE OF THE BOOK

As a springboard for success, this book, *Leading with Emotional Intelligence: A Guide for Board Directors*, was written to serve as an all-encompassing resource for board directors interested in cultivating their emotional intelligence. Its purpose is to educate directors on what emotional intelligence is, highlight its significance, and offer guidance on its further development.

Robert K. Cooper (1997) once said, "Emotional intelligence is the ability to sense, understand, and effectively apply the power and acumen of emotions as a source of human energy, information, connection, and influence." And that is exactly what happens in the boardroom; beyond the corporate processes, professional interactions, and actions guided by numbers, we are still all humans.

The increasing integration of artificial intelligence (AI) and automation in the professional landscape has necessitated a pertinent discussion about the importance of emotional intelligence as a "must-have" skill. As routine tasks and jobs are being replaced by technology, the uniquely human qualities associated with emotional intelligence are becoming more valuable than ever.

In addition to the standard criteria for sharp business acumen and strong business credentials, board directors who are also emotionally intelligent are in a prime position to steer their companies to success.

Moving forward, this book provides actionable tips and tactics for using emotional intelligence in the boardroom, such as methods for making sound decisions, resolving conflicts, improving communication, and building strong relationships with colleagues. It also emphasizes the value of emotional intelligence in the boardroom, where directors must balance the needs of various stakeholders, navigate complex issues, and foster a collaborative culture to boost productivity.

INTRODUCTION

In today's ever-evolving business landscape, the role of board directors has transformed significantly. Beyond making strategic decisions and ensuring fiduciary responsibilities, board directors are now expected to demonstrate exceptional leadership qualities that go beyond mere intellect and experience. To truly drive organizational success, board directors must master the art of a deep understanding of emotions, empathy, and the ability to connect with others on a profound level.

Leading with Emotional Intelligence: A Guide for Board Directors is a transformative resource that equips directors with the essential tools to navigate the complexities of modern governance through the lens of emotional intelligence.

Emotional intelligence, often referred to as EI or EQ, encompasses a set of skills that enable individuals to recognize, understand, and manage their own emotions, as well as the emotions of others. It provides a framework for effective communication, collaboration, and decision-making.

In the context of board governance, emotional intelligence is an indispensable attribute that can foster trust, strengthen relationships, and guide ethical leadership.

Leading with Emotional Intelligence: A Guide for Board Directors delves into the intersection of emotional intelligence and boardroom leadership, offering valuable insights, practical strategies, and actionable steps for board directors to enhance their effectiveness and lead with purpose.

In **Chapter 1**, readers embark on a journey to unravel the intricate nature of emotions and emotional intelligence, and their relevance in the boardroom. It discusses the profound impact of emotions on human behavior, decision-making, and interpersonal relationships.

In addition, this chapter delves into the concept of heart intelligence, which goes beyond cognitive intelligence and taps into the power of the heart as a source of wisdom and intuition. It emphasizes the role of emotions in decision-making, highlighting the importance of listening to one's inner guidance and cultivating emotional authenticity in leadership roles. Readers will learn strategies to develop heart intelligence and leverage its transformative potential in the boardroom.

Chapter 2 provides a comprehensive overview of the five key components of emotional intelligence: self-awareness, self-regulation, motivation, empathy, and social skills. Through real-life examples and practical exercises, board directors can gain insights into developing and enhancing each component, equipping them with the emotional intelligence toolkit needed to lead effectively in the boardroom.

Furthermore, the chapter explores the unique challenges and opportunities that board directors face in leading with emotional intelligence. It addresses topics such as managing conflict, navigating diversity and inclusion, and fostering a culture of trust and accountability. Readers will learn how emotional intelligence can serve as a powerful tool in addressing these challenges and cultivating a positive boardroom environment that fosters collaboration and drives organizational success.

Chapter 3 brings emotional intelligence to life within the context of the boardroom. From strategic leadership and decision-making to stakeholder engagement and succession planning, readers will discover how emotional intelligence can elevate their effectiveness in these crucial areas.

Lastly, **Chapter 4** challenges traditional notions of governance and highlights the need for an evolved approach in the modern business landscape. Readers will discover how emotional intelligence can reshape governance practices and promote transparency, accountability, and ethical decision-making in alignment with the evolving needs of stakeholders and society.

Beyond being a simple guide, this book introduces a transformative journey. It seeks to navigate directors through the subtleties of emotional intelligence, from the individual nuances of empathy and self-awareness to their larger implications on organizational health and resilience. It addresses complex boardroom dynamics and presents innovative ways to enhance collective decision-making while fostering an environment of mutual respect and understanding.

Each chapter combines theoretical knowledge with practical guidance, offering strategies and techniques to leverage emotional intelligence for optimal boardroom leadership.

This book is a valuable resource for board directors, executives, and anyone seeking to enhance their leadership abilities through the power of emotional intelligence. By embarking on this journey, readers will gain the insights, tools, and strategies to elevate their leadership presence, cultivate meaningful relationships, and shape a future where emotional intelligence is at the heart of effective governance.

Chapter 1

UNDERSTANDING
EMOTIONAL INTELLIGENCE

Unveiling the Essence of Emotional Intelligence

"Knowing yourself is the beginning
of all wisdom."
— Aristotle

Emotional intelligence is a term used to encompass a set of skills that enable individuals to recognize, understand, and manage their own emotions and the emotions of others. It goes beyond mere intellect or academic achievements, delving into the realm of understanding and managing emotions, both within ourselves and in our interactions with others. It entails a repertoire of abilities that empower individuals to adeptly navigate social interactions, demonstrate empathy towards others, effectively regulate their own emotions, and make informed decisions by attuning to emotional cues.

Emotional intelligence has emerged as a critical construct in understanding human behavior and success in various domains. More than just being aware of our feelings, emotional intelligence involves effectively utilizing our emotions to guide our thoughts, behavior, and decision-making processes. It empowers individuals to navigate the complexities of life with wisdom and compassion.

By delving into the realm of emotional intelligence, individuals open themselves to a deeper understanding of the intricate interplay between emotions, cognition, and interpersonal relationships. This exploration invites them to discover the realms of self-awareness, self-regulation, empathy, and social skills. Understanding emotional intelligence not only enables individuals to navigate their own emotional landscapes with grace and resilience, but also equips them with invaluable tools to forge deeper connections, enhance communication, and lead more fulfilling and successful lives.

The essence of emotional intelligence lies in its transformative power. It enables individuals to regulate their emotions effectively, making them resilient in the face of adversity. Emotionally intelligent individuals have the ability to manage stress, control impulses, adapt to change, remain calm and composed, and make well-informed decisions, even in challenging situations. They can find it easier to maintain a positive mindset, seek opportunities for growth, and bounce back from setbacks with determination. Consequently, grasping the significance of emotional intelligence is paramount.

In the forthcoming chapters, we will embark on a captivating journey to unravel the essence of emotional intelligence, delving into its intricate nature and multifaceted components.

Mayer and Salovey (1997) introduced the concept of emotional intelligence as a distinct form of intelligence. They proposed a model of emotional intelligence consisting of four components: perceiving emotions, using emotions to facilitate thinking, understanding emotions, and managing emotions. According to their research, individuals with higher emotional intelligence tend to have better interpersonal relationships, cope with stress more effectively, and demonstrate higher levels of overall well-being.

Goleman (1995) expanded on this model and introduced the concept of emotional intelligence in leadership. His research highlighted that leaders with higher emotional intelligence exhibit better self-awareness, empathy, and interpersonal skills, leading to enhanced team performance and organizational outcomes. Goleman also proposed that EI is a more accurate predictor of success than traditional measures of intelligence, and delineated five fundamental elements comprising emotional intelligence.

The five key components of emotional intelligence (according to Goleman) are:

1. **Self-awareness:** The ability to recognize and understand one's own emotions, values, strengths and weaknesses. Self-aware individuals are attuned to their emotional state and can accurately assess their thoughts and behavior.

2. **Self-regulation:** Refers to the ability to manage and control

one's emotions, impulses, and behaviors in appropriate ways. This includes managing stress, adapting to change, and maintaining emotional stability in challenging situations.

3. **Motivation:** Motivation in the context of emotional intelligence refers to the ability to channel emotions toward achieving personal and professional goals. Individuals with high emotional intelligence are self-driven, resilient, and able to maintain a positive attitude even in the face of setbacks.

4. **Social awareness / empathy:** This involves understanding and sharing the emotions of others. It allows individuals to perceive and respond to the feelings and needs of others, fostering better interpersonal relationships and effective communication.

5. **Relationship management / social skills:** Social skills encompass a range of abilities, including effective communication, conflict resolution, teamwork, and leadership. Those with developed social skills can build and maintain strong relationships, influence others positively, and navigate social dynamics adeptly.

Extensive research has been conducted to understand the impact of emotional intelligence on various aspects of life. Numerous studies have highlighted the benefits of high emotional intelligence in personal and professional domains.

In the workplace, employees with high emotional intelligence exhibit better job performance, leadership skills, and decision-making abilities. A meta-analysis conducted by Joseph and Newman (2010) found a significant correlation between emotional intelligence and job performance across different industries and occupations.

Additionally, employees with higher EI are more likely to display organizational citizenship behaviors, such as helping colleagues and going beyond their job requirements. This notion was substantiated by Côté and Miners (2006), who also discovered a positive association between emotional intelligence and job performance.

Emotional intelligence plays a vital role in leadership effectiveness. A study by Boyatzis, Smith, and Blaize (2006) found that leaders with higher emotional intelligence positively influenced employee engagement, job satisfaction, and overall team performance. Leaders who demonstrate empathy, self-awareness, and strong interpersonal skills create a supportive and collaborative work environment that fosters creativity, innovation, and productivity.

In the realm of education, research suggests that emotional intelligence contributes to academic success. A study by Brackett, Rivers, and Salovey (2011) found that students with higher emotional intelligence demonstrated better academic achievement, stronger social relationships, and fewer behavioral problems. They found that EI skills, such as self-regulation and empathy, enhanced students' ability to manage stress, cope with challenges, and build positive relationships with peers and teachers.

Furthermore, emotional intelligence has a profound impact on personal relationships and overall well-being. Individuals with higher EI experience more satisfying and fulfilling relationships, better communication, and higher levels of empathy. A study conducted by Ciarrochi, Deane and Anderson (2002) found that emotional intelligence was positively associated with various aspects of relationship dynamics, including relationship satisfaction, conflict resolution skills, and overall relationship quality.

Similarly, another study by Brackett and Mayer (2003) explored the relationship between emotional intelligence and life satisfaction. The findings indicated that individuals with higher emotional intelligence tend to experience greater life satisfaction and overall well-being.

Research also shows that individuals with high emotional intelligence have lower levels of stress, anxiety, and depression. They possess effective coping strategies and are better equipped to manage challenging situations.

Emotional intelligence is particularly important in the boardroom, where relationships between board directors and the executive leadership team can be intricate and intense. Board directors who possess advanced emotional intelligence are more adept at cultivating trust, handling conflicts, and reaching decisions that yield overall benefits to the organization.

Previous studies substantiate that boards with elevated emotional intelligence skills are more inclined to attain their strategic objectives and excel in their performance. Research for Vantage Circle (2023) supports these claims, finding that emotional intelligence has an influence of 58% on job performance. In a striking display of commitment to this concept, some companies have even embraced the integration of emotional intelligence assessments within their recruitment and evaluation processes.

Emotional intelligence is not an immutable trait, but a dynamic attribute that can be nurtured and refined over time through deliberate practice and introspection. By prioritizing emotional intelligence in their interactions and actively striving to improve their skills in this domain, board directors possess the capacity to propel their organizations towards thriving success.

Significance of Emotional Intelligence in Corporate Governance

Corporate governance plays a crucial role in the success and effectiveness of an organization. Emotional intelligence has gained increasing recognition as a critical factor in effective corporate governance. Corporate leaders are expected to possess not only technical expertise but also strong emotional intelligence skills.

Emotional intelligence is often mistakenly labeled as a mere "soft skill," implying that it is secondary to technical expertise or strategic acumen. However, research and real-world experiences have consistently shown that EI is far from being just a nice-to-have attribute; it is a critical competency that drives leadership effectiveness and shapes the dynamics within the boardroom.

In the wake of rising technology and artificial intelligence, emotional intelligence is vital for board directors, particularly in terms of fostering critical thinking and decision-making. As technology continues to advance and reshape industries, board directors must navigate the complexities of digital transformations, emerging risks, and the ethical implications of AI. Emotional intelligence becomes a crucial competency that enhances their ability to lead effectively and make informed decisions.

Technology and AI excel in tasks that require logical reasoning, data analysis, and problem-solving based on predetermined algorithms. Emotionally intelligent directors, however, have the capacity to analyze these inputs through a human lens, considering the broader implications for stakeholders, employees, and wider society. They can recognize potential biases or ethical concerns and approach decision-making with a balanced perspective, weighing both logical and emotional factors.

Additionally, emotional intelligence enhances the ability to manage the uncertainties and disruptions associated with technological advancements. As boards navigate complex strategic decisions, emotionally intelligent directors can empathize with the concerns and anxieties of employees and stakeholders. They can effectively communicate the rationale behind technology-driven changes, addressing emotional reactions and providing reassurance. Emotional intelligence helps directors build trust, promote open dialogue, and foster collaboration within the boardroom, leading to better decision outcomes.

Moreover, emotional intelligence is essential for addressing the ethical dimensions of technology and AI. As these technologies become more integrated into our lives, board directors must grapple with issues such as data privacy, algorithmic biases, and the potential displacement of workers. Emotional intelligence allows directors to consider the ethical implications of these developments, ensuring that decisions align with organizational values and broader societal interests. This can be achieved through actively engaging in discussions about the responsible use of technology, advocating for transparency, and providing guidance on the ethical frameworks necessary to navigate the evolving technological landscape.

Leadership effectiveness is another domain where emotional intelligence proves indispensable. Leadership effectiveness hinges on the ability to navigate complex human interactions, inspire and motivate others, and make sound decisions that consider the broader impact on individuals and teams. These qualities are deeply rooted in emotional intelligence.

Leaders with high EI possess self-awareness, allowing them to understand their strengths, weaknesses, and emotional triggers. This self-awareness enables them to regulate their own emotions, maintain composure under pressure, and project a sense of authenticity and empathy. By connecting with and understanding the emotions of their team members, emotionally intelligent leaders can build trust, foster engagement, and inspire higher levels of performance.

Effective corporate governance relies on strong leadership. A study by Cherniss and Goleman (2001) examined the impact of emotional intelligence on leadership performance and identified a direct relationship between the two. The study demonstrated that leaders with higher emotional intelligence were more likely to inspire and motivate employees, foster collaboration, and navigate complex interpersonal dynamics. Their ability to empathize and understand the emotions of others enabled them to build trust, enhance team cohesion, and facilitate effective communication.

In the realm of corporate governance, emotional intelligence also emphasizes the significance of interpersonal dynamics and the emotional dimensions that shape interactions within the boardroom. In the confines of the boardroom, when directors understand their own emotions and how they affect their behavior, they can better control their reactions in high-pressure situations. This can help with conflict avoidance and building stronger relationships with their colleagues.

This is where EI becomes invaluable. It enables individuals to navigate the complexities of human interactions, build meaningful relationships, and demonstrate empathy and understanding—qualities that are inherently human and difficult to replicate in machines.

Furthermore, emotional intelligence positively influences overall boardroom dynamics. A boardroom characterized by a high level of emotional intelligence fosters an inclusive and psychologically safe environment, where individuals feel comfortable expressing their ideas, challenging assumptions, and sharing dissenting opinions. This encourages healthy debate, innovative thinking, and better decision-making.

Emotionally intelligent board members also exhibit strong interpersonal skills, such as active listening and empathy, which facilitate effective communication and build cohesive relationships among board members.

Eisenbeiss, Knippenberg, and Boerner (2008) suggest that emotional intelligence enhances interpersonal relationships within the boardroom. Directors with high emotional intelligence are more likely to demonstrate conflict resolution skills, leading to constructive board discussions and decision-making. This fosters a culture of trust, respect, and open communication among board members, ultimately enhancing governance effectiveness.

Numerous studies have explored the link between emotional intelligence and board effectiveness. Research by Van Kleef, De Dreu, and Manstead (2010) demonstrates that emotionally intelligent board directors are more effective in managing boardroom dynamics and fostering positive relationships. When they exhibit empathy and social awareness, emotionally intelligent directors create an inclusive and collaborative boardroom environment that positively impacts teamwork, communication, and decision-making.

Board directors are responsible for making decisions that will shape the future of their organization. In order to make effective decisions, they need to be able to work well with their fellow board directors, the CEO, the executive team, and other stakeholders. This is why emotional intelligence is so important. According to research undertaken by Stanford Research Institute International and the Carnegie Melon Foundation, among Fortune 500 CEOs, interpersonal abilities account for 75% of long-term professional success, while technical knowledge accounts for only 25% (Pairin n.d.). Directors with high emotional intelligence are better equipped to consider and manage their own emotions, as well as understand and respond to the emotions of others. This enables them to make more informed decisions that consider both the business implications and the potential impact on stakeholders.

Effective corporate governance requires engaging and understanding the needs and perspectives of various stakeholders. Emotional intelligence plays a vital role in this process. Research by Dulewicz and Herbert (2004) suggests that emotionally intelligent board directors possess better interpersonal skills, allowing them to establish rapport, build trust, and effectively communicate with stakeholders. Applying empathy and active listening, emotionally intelligent directors demonstrate a genuine understanding of stakeholder concerns and values, leading to enhanced relationships and sustainable stakeholder engagement.

Ethics and integrity are integral to corporate governance. Emotional intelligence contributes to ethical decision-making by enabling board directors to navigate complex ethical dilemmas with integrity and fairness. Research by Treviño, Butterfield, and McCabe (1998) indicates that emotionally intelligent individuals are more likely to consider moral implications and exhibit ethical behavior. Emotionally intelligent directors possess a heightened sense of self-awareness, allowing them to manage personal biases and make principled decisions that align with the organization's values and long-term sustainability. Individuals with higher emotional intelligence exhibit greater moral reasoning and are more likely to consider ethical implications in their decision-making processes.

Emotional intelligence has a profound impact on long-term organizational performance. Research by Boyatzis, Goleman, and Rhee (2000) indicates a positive association between emotional intelligence and leadership effectiveness, employee engagement, and overall organizational success. Emotionally intelligent board directors are skilled at inspiring and motivating others, fostering a culture of innovation and adapting to changing market conditions.

> "If your emotional abilities aren't in hand, if you don't have self-awareness, if you are not able to manage your distressing emotions, if you can't have empathy and have effective relationships, then no matter how smart you are, you are not going to get very far."
> – Daniel Goleman

Drawing on the above-mentioned research, the benefits of emotional intelligence for board directors can be summarized as follows:

Connecting with team members: Directors with a high level of emotional intelligence can form deeper connections with their peers. A leader's ability to keep their composure under pressure increases when they deeply understand their own emotions and how they affect their behavior. Directors will have a more significant opportunity for peaceful conflict resolution and the development of solid professional relationships if they choose this course of action.

Emotional understanding and awareness: Directors with high emotional intelligence also better grasp the feelings of others around them. Individuals who can put themselves in their colleagues' shoes can better see things from their peers' points of view and come up with collaborative solutions. This has the potential to lead to more effective collaboration and outstanding results for the company as a whole.

Cultivating a culture of respect: Gaining the respect of one's fellow board members is yet another way in which emotional intelligence benefits directors. Recognizing and controlling one's own emotions makes one more trustworthy and dependable. Eventually, this may improve their communication and rapport with their peers, leading to more effective collaboration.

Thoughtful choices: Awareness of oneself and emotional stability increase resilience against prejudice and other outside effects. Directors will be better equipped to make objective decisions for the betterment of the entire business entity.

Emotional intelligence is of utmost significance in corporate governance as it influences decision-making, leadership effectiveness, board dynamics, ethical conduct, and organizational outcomes. Directors with high emotional intelligence possess the skills necessary to navigate complex business challenges, build strong relationships, and make ethical and informed decisions.

By recognizing the importance of emotional intelligence and fostering its development within the boardroom, organizations can enhance governance effectiveness and drive sustainable success.

To gain a comprehensive understanding of emotional intelligence, it is essential to first comprehend the nature of emotions.

Unraveling the Essence of Emotions

" To find yourself, think for yourself."
— Socrates

Emotions are a fundamental aspect of human experience, influencing an individual's thoughts, behavior, and overall well-being. Despite their ubiquitous presence, defining and understanding emotions remains a complex and multidimensional task. Extensive research has shed light on the nature and mechanisms of emotions, providing valuable insights into their profound impact on human cognition and behavior.

Emotions can be defined as complex psychological and physiological states that arise in response to internal or external stimuli, shaping an individual's subjective experience and influencing their behavior (Ekman 1999). Emotions encompass a wide range of affective experiences, such as happiness, sadness, anger, fear, and disgust.

While emotions are universally experienced, their expression and interpretation may vary due to cultural perceptions and individual differences (Mesquita & Albert 2007).

Emotions consist of various components that work in harmony to create the overall emotional experience. The cognitive component involves the appraisal and interpretation of a situation, leading to the generation of an emotional response (Lazarus 1991). The physiological component involves changes in bodily responses, including heart rate, hormonal secretions, and facial expressions (Levenson 1999). The subjective component refers to the subjective experience of an emotion, including the feeling of pleasure or displeasure associated with it (James 1884). These components collectively contribute to the holistic experience of an emotion.

Numerous theories have been proposed to explain the nature and mechanisms of emotions. The James-Lange theory suggests that physiological responses precede and give rise to the experience of emotions (James 1884). Conversely, the Cannon-Bard theory proposes that emotions and physiological responses occur simultaneously and independently (Cannon 1927). The cognitive appraisal theory emphasizes the role of cognitive evaluations in shaping emotional experiences (Lazarus 1991). It proposes that individuals' emotional responses to situations are determined by their subjective evaluations and interpretations of those situations. Additionally, the facial feedback hypothesis suggests that changes in facial expressions can influence emotional experiences (Strack, Martin & Stepper 1988).

These theories offer valuable insights into the complexities of emotions, highlighting the intricate interplay between cognitive, physiological, and subjective factors.

Neural Mechanisms of Emotions

According to the findings of Ekman and Davidson (1994), emotions involve both automatic and controlled processes. Automatic processes, driven by subcortical brain regions, trigger immediate physiological changes, such as increased heart rate and facial expressions. Controlled processes, originating from cortical areas, involve conscious cognitive appraisal, interpretation, and regulation of emotions.

Advancements in neuroscience have provided further valuable insights into the neural mechanisms underlying emotions. Research using brain imaging techniques, such as functional magnetic resonance imaging (fMRI), has identified key brain regions involved in emotional processing.

The amygdala plays a crucial role in the evaluation of emotional stimuli and the generation of emotional responses (LeDoux 2000). The amygdala rapidly assesses emotional significance, determining the appropriate emotional response and triggering a cascade of physiological and behavioral reactions. The prefrontal cortex, particularly the ventromedial prefrontal cortex, is involved in the regulation and modulation of emotions (Ochsner & Gross 2005). Additionally, the insula is implicated in the subjective experience of emotions (Craig 2009).

These findings highlight the intricate neural circuitry that underlies emotional processes.

Emotions play a vital role in overall well-being and psychological functioning. Positive emotions, such as happiness and joy, are associated with improved mental health, resilience, and social connectedness (Fredrickson 2001). Negative emotions, such as sadness and anger, can serve as adaptive responses to threats or injustices, though chronic or intense negative emotions may contribute to mental health disorders (Kring & Sloan 2009).

Emotional regulation—the ability to modulate and manage emotions effectively—is crucial for maintaining psychological well-being (Gross 2015). Developing emotional intelligence and adaptive coping strategies can enhance emotional regulation skills and promote well-being.

Function and Importance of Emotions

Emotions serve crucial adaptive functions, aiding in survival, social bonding, and decision-making processes.

One primary function of emotions is to provide us with valuable information about ourselves and our environment. Emotions act as signals, alerting us to our needs, desires, and potential threats. Evolutionary theories propose that emotions have evolved to guide behavior in response to environmental challenges and opportunities (Tooby & Cosmides 2008). For instance, the emotion of fear prompts individuals to escape or avoid potential threats, thereby enhancing chances of survival.

Emotions also play a fundamental role in social interactions. Ekman (2003) highlights the communicative function of emotions, where facial expressions, vocal cues, and body language transmit emotional information to others—thereby fostering empathy, cooperation, and social cohesion. Emotional expressions allow individuals to understand and respond to the emotional states of others, facilitating effective interpersonal relationships. For example, emotional expressions, such as laughter or tears, serve as social cues, conveying information about our internal states to those around us.

Emotions also contribute to our overall well-being and mental health. By acknowledging and expressing our emotions, we can process and release them in a healthy way. Suppressing or denying emotions can lead to emotional distress and potential long-term negative effects on our mental and physical health. Emotions offer us an opportunity for self-reflection and growth, guiding us towards a more balanced and authentic existence.

Additionally, emotions significantly influence cognitive processes and decision-making. Damasio's somatic marker hypothesis (1994) proposes that emotions provide rapid, intuitive signals that guide decision-making by integrating emotional experiences with cognitive evaluations. Emotions shape our preferences, biases, and risk perception, influencing choices and behavior. They act as a compass, helping us evaluate options and make choices that align with our values and desires. By tapping into our emotional responses, we gain insights into what resonates with us on a deeper level; therefore, emotions can serve as powerful motivators, driving us to pursue our goals and aspirations.

Emotions are not solely driven by internal processes but are also shaped by social and cultural factors. Research suggests that cultural norms and values influence the ways in which emotions are experienced, expressed, and regulated (Matsumoto 2006). Moreover, social interactions and relationships significantly impact emotional experiences, as emotions serve as a means of communication, social bonding, and empathy (Gottman & Levenson 1992).

As outlined, emotions have a profound impact on our decision-making processes, shaping the choices we make and the actions we take. However, it is crucial to recognize that our past traumatic experiences, cultural influences, and biases can significantly influence our emotional responses, leading to potentially biased or irrational decision-making. This is where emotional intelligence and understanding our emotions become critical. By developing emotional intelligence, we gain a deeper understanding of the underlying factors that contribute to our emotional responses, allowing us to make more informed and rational decisions.

Traumatic experiences from our past can shape our emotional landscape. Unresolved trauma can result in heightened emotional reactions or trigger specific emotional patterns that may not be proportionate to the present situation. For example, an individual who has experienced a traumatic event in the past may exhibit intense fear or anxiety in similar situations, even if the present circumstances do not warrant such a strong emotional response. Recognizing and understanding the influence of past trauma on our emotions helps us separate the present reality from the unresolved emotions of the past, enabling more balanced decision-making.

Cultural and societal influences also shape our emotional responses and decision-making. Each culture has different norms, values, and expectations which influence the way we perceive and express emotions. For example, in some cultures, displaying vulnerability or sadness may be considered undesirable, leading individuals to suppress or deny these emotions. Conversely, in other cultures, certain emotions may be encouraged or even expected in specific situations. Understanding the cultural context and biases that shape our emotional responses enables us to examine and challenge their influence on our decision-making, promoting balanced and unbiased choices.

Prejudice, both conscious and unconscious, can also color our emotional experiences and decision-making processes. Preconceived notions and biases based on race, gender, religion, or other social identities can trigger emotions such as anger, resentment, or fear, which can in turn affect our judgment. These biases can lead to unfair treatment, stereotyping, discriminatory behavior, flawed decision-making, or the overlooking of important information and perspectives.

By developing emotional intelligence, we become more aware of the impact of cultural and societal influences on our emotions. We can then challenge and critically evaluate our own biases, fostering more inclusive and equitable decision-making processes.

Emotional intelligence not only helps us understand our emotions, but also equips us with the tools to manage them effectively. Self-regulation, a key aspect of emotional intelligence, enables us to control impulsive emotional reactions and make decisions based on a broader perspective. By managing our emotions, we can reduce the risk of making rash or regrettable decisions driven solely by intense emotional states.

Furthermore, emotional intelligence enhances our ability to empathize with others through recognizing and understanding their emotions and perspectives. Empathy allows us to consider the impact of our decisions on others and make choices that are not solely self-centered. It fosters better communication, collaboration, and conflict resolution, promoting harmonious relationships and a more inclusive decision-making process.

Developing emotional intelligence is a lifelong journey that requires self-reflection, self-awareness, and a willingness to grow. It involves becoming attuned to our emotional triggers, understanding the reasons behind our emotional responses, and practicing self-regulation techniques to manage them effectively. Seeking support from therapists, coaches, or mentors can also be beneficial in exploring past traumas, addressing biases, and developing emotional intelligence.

Embracing Heart Intelligence and Inner Wisdom

"My business skills have come from being guided by my inner self – my intuition."
– Oprah Winfrey

Heart intelligence, also known as "heart coherence," refers to the idea that the heart possesses its own unique intelligence and plays a crucial role in individuals' overall well-being and decision-making processes. It goes beyond conventional notions of intelligence based solely on cognitive abilities and emphasizes the importance of emotions, intuition, and the energetic qualities of the heart.

At the core of heart intelligence is the recognition that the heart is not just a physical organ, but also an information processing center. It has its own intricate network of neurons, neurotransmitters, and sensory receptors which enables it to communicate with the brain and other systems in the body. This communication occurs through the autonomic nervous system, hormonal signals, and electromagnetic signals emitted by the heart.

Heart intelligence is closely linked to emotions, as the heart is considered a key center for experiencing and processing emotions, which influence one's perceptions, judgments, and behaviors. When people experience positive emotions like love, care, gratitude, and compassion, the heart's electromagnetic field becomes more coherent and harmonious, positively affecting their overall well-being. Conversely, negative emotions such as anger, fear, and stress can disrupt the heart's coherence and have detrimental effects on one's health and decision-making abilities.

Studies have shown that when individuals are in a state of heart coherence, characterized by a harmonious heart rhythm pattern, they experience a range of benefits, such as improved cognitive performance, enhanced creativity, increased emotional resilience, and more effective communication and relationships.

One study conducted by McCraty et al. (2009) explored the relationship between heart coherence and cognitive performance. The findings revealed that individuals in a state of heart coherence demonstrated improved cognitive performance, including enhanced memory, attention, and problem-solving abilities. This suggests that the heart's coherent rhythm positively influences cognitive functions.

Practices such as heart-focused breathing, meditation, and cultivating positive emotions can help individuals attain heart coherence and develop their heart intelligence. Heart coherence techniques involve consciously directing attention to the area of the heart, breathing deeply and rhythmically, and focusing on positive feelings or emotions. These practices help synchronize the heart's rhythms, enhance its coherence, and promote a state of inner balance and alignment.

One of the significant benefits of heart intelligence is its impact on decision-making. When individuals tap into their heart intelligence, they gain access to a profound level of wisdom and intuition. The heart has been described as a source of intuitive guidance, providing insights and guidance beyond what can be obtained through logical analysis alone. By integrating heart intelligence into their decision-making processes, individuals can make choices that are in alignment with their values, intuition, and the well-being of themselves and others.

Furthermore, heart intelligence plays a crucial role in fostering social coherence and harmonious relationships. The electromagnetic field generated by the heart can interact with the fields of other individuals, influencing their emotional states and communication. When individuals are in a state of heart coherence, they radiate positive and coherent energy, which can have a ripple effect, promoting empathy, understanding, and cooperation within social interactions and groups.

"The heart is forever making the head its fool."
- Kahlil Gibran

Incorporating heart intelligence into various aspects of life, including personal relationships, leadership, and organizational culture, can lead to profound transformations. It enables individuals to cultivate compassion and resilience, fostering a more harmonious and compassionate society.

Enhancing Decision-Making through Instinctive Insights

Heart intelligence and intuition are closely interconnected, working in harmony to enhance our understanding of ourselves and the world around us.

Intuition is a powerful and often subconscious process that influences our decision-making abilities. It is often described as a form of knowing that arises without conscious reasoning or logical explanation. It can manifest as a feeling, a hunch, or a sense of certainty about a particular situation or decision.

Intuition is not limited to the realm of emotions; it draws on a vast array of unconscious knowledge and experiences that our rational mind may not be able to access. Many successful individuals attribute their achievements to the trust they place in their intuition. Steve Jobs, for instance, famously stated, "Intuition is a very powerful thing; more powerful than intellect."

The Science of Intuition

While intuition is sometimes dismissed as a vague or unreliable source of information, numerous studies have highlighted its value in decision-making. For example, Gigerenzer and Gaissmaier (2011) found that in certain situations, relying on intuitive judgments can lead to faster and more accurate decision-making compared to extensive analysis.

Intuition can provide a holistic understanding of complex situations, drawing on tacit knowledge and pattern recognition that may not be readily accessible to conscious reasoning.

"Intuition is not the enemy, but
the ally, of reason."
– John Kord Lagemann

Furthermore, intuition can be particularly useful when making complex choices and in situations characterized by uncertainty or time constraints. Through a series of experiments, Dijksterhuis and Nordgren (2006) demonstrated that individuals who relied on their intuition performed better than those who engaged in deliberate analysis. This suggests that intuition can be an efficient and effective tool for decision-making, especially when immediate action is required or when the available information on which to base the decision is limited.

The neurobiological basis of intuition has also been explored. Studies using fMRI brain imaging techniques have shown that intuitive decisions are associated with increased activity in the emotional and intuitive areas of the brain, such as the ventromedial prefrontal cortex (Bechara et al. 1997). This suggests that intuition involves a combination of cognitive and emotional processes, allowing us to tap into a deeper understanding beyond conscious reasoning.

Intuition (often described as a "gut feeling") is a powerful tool that can help board members make better decisions and create lasting change, particularly in the areas of creativity, innovation, and problem-solving. It is a skill that can be developed through practice and experience.

"The intuitive mind is a sacred gift and the rational mind is a faithful servant. We have created a society that honors the servant and has forgotten the gift."
— Albert Einstein

Here are some basics of intuition that board members should keep in mind:

Trusting one's instincts is crucial: The individual's intuition serves as an inner voice that offers guidance during decision-making processes. It is vital to have faith in one's instincts and pay attention to that inner voice. Frequently, intuition provides insights that may go unnoticed by the conscious mind.

Paying attention to one's emotions is essential: Emotions serve as a potent source of information, offering valuable clues about what truly matters and warrants attention. By being attuned to their emotions, directors can access their intuition more effectively and make improved decisions.

Practicing mindfulness is recommended: Mindfulness entails being fully present in the current moment, without passing judgment. This powerful practice enables individuals to enhance their awareness of their thoughts and emotions. By engaging in mindfulness, a deeper comprehension of one's intuition can be cultivated, fostering increased trust in its guidance.

The practice of visualization is emphasized: Visualization is a powerful tool that enables individuals to access their intuition effectively. It entails mentally envisioning a particular situation or desired outcome, then allowing one's intuition to provide guidance towards that objective. By incorporating visualization into their routine, directors can bolster their confidence in their intuition and make enhanced decisions.

Taking action is critical: Intuition encompasses more than just having insights; it also involves actively pursuing and implementing those insights. Once individuals have a strong gut feeling about something, it becomes crucial to take decisive action and follow through. This approach can serve as a powerful catalyst for creating lasting change and making a tangible impact.

However, it is important to note that intuition is not infallible and can be influenced by biases or unreliable information. This is the critical juncture where emotional intelligence and self-awareness of biases become significant factors. A balanced approach that integrates both rational analysis and intuition is often recommended for decision-making. By combining conscious deliberation with intuitive insights, directors can leverage the strengths of both approaches and make more well-rounded and informed decisions.

Exploring the Intertwined Nature of Intuition and Emotional Intelligence

"Trust your hunches. They' re usually based
on facts filed away just below the
conscious level."
— Joyce Brothers

In recent years, there has been a growing recognition of the importance of emotional intelligence and intuition in various aspects of life, including personal relationships, professional success, and overall well-being. While these two concepts are often discussed separately, they are closely related and work together to provide a holistic understanding of a situation, empowering individuals to make decisions that are not only rational but also empathetic and compassionate.

EI and intuition can be seen as different aspects of a broader concept known as "heart intelligence." Heart intelligence encompasses the integration of emotions, intuition, and rational thinking, allowing individuals to make wise decisions, build meaningful connections, and live with greater authenticity.

Several studies have shed light on the interconnectedness of intuition and emotional intelligence. In a study by Salovey, Mayer, and Caruso (2009), participants were assessed on measures of emotional intelligence and intuitive decision-making. The results indicated a positive correlation between emotional intelligence and intuitive decision-making, suggesting that individuals with higher emotional intelligence were more likely to rely on their intuition in decision-making processes.

Emotional intelligence plays a vital role in recognizing and comprehending the emotions connected to intuition, facilitating a more effective interpretation and response. Through emotional awareness, individuals can discern between fear-driven resistance and authentic intuitive guidance. By nurturing emotional intelligence, individuals enhance their ability to navigate the intricacies of their emotions and make decisions that are aligned with their profound intuition.

Cultivating heart intelligence and nurturing intuition and emotional intelligence requires intentional practice and self-awareness. However, if this is done successfully, directors can tap into their intuitive insights and emotional wisdom. Likewise, embracing the interconnectedness of heart intelligence, intuition, and emotional intelligence can lead to greater self-awareness, authentic connections with others, and a more balanced approach to life's challenges.

To encourage heart intelligence, board members must learn to trust their intuition and use it alongside their intellectual intelligence. This means creating a safe and supportive environment where directors feel comfortable sharing their thoughts and feelings, and where intuition is valued as much as data and logic—something which is unfortunately often overlooked in boardroom environments that prioritize logic and data-driven approaches.

It also means recognizing the importance of empathy and emotional intelligence in building strong relationships with stakeholders, employees, and customers.

Crucially, emotional intelligence is not just about being "nice" or "friendly". It encompasses a profound awareness of one's own emotions and biases, as well as those of others, and using that awareness to make better decisions.

Having explored the nature of emotions and their pivotal role in decision-making, we will uncover the detrimental consequences of neglecting emotions in the work environment and pave the way for a more holistic and effective approach to organizational decision-making.

Neglecting Emotions in the Professional Environment: The Critical Influence on Decision-Making

"The intellect has little to do on the road to discovery. There comes a leap in consciousness, call it Intuition or what you will, the solution comes to you and you don't know how or why."
– Albert Einstein

Emotions play a crucial role in shaping one's thoughts, behaviors, and decision-making processes. However, in the professional environment, emotions are often neglected or dismissed as irrelevant factors.

The traditional belief that human decision-making is purely rational, guided by logical thinking and careful analysis, has been challenged by emerging research indicating that humans make decisions emotionally, and subsequently employ their rational mind to justify those choices.

For example, research in psychology and neuroscience consistently demonstrates that emotions significantly influence decision-making. Damasio's somatic marker hypothesis proposes that emotions act as signals that guide decision-making by providing positive or negative valence to potential options (Damasio 1994). This emotional valence serves as a heuristic or shortcut that helps individuals quickly assess and select from available choices. Numerous studies have shown that emotions influence risk perception, motivation, and preference formation, thus shaping the ultimate decision outcome (Lerner & Keltner 2000; Loewenstein et al. 2001).

Neuroimaging studies provide evidence of the brain's involvement in emotional decision-making. The amygdala, a key structure involved in processing emotions, has been found to play a crucial role in decision-making. Bechara et al. (1997) conducted a study involving patients with damage to the amygdala and found that they exhibited impaired decision-making, particularly in situations involving emotionally charged stimuli. This suggests that emotions, as processed by the amygdala, are essential for adaptive decision-making.

After making a decision based on emotions, individuals often engage in post-decisional rationalization to justify their choices. Kunda's motivated reasoning theory suggests that people actively search for and generate reasons to support their decisions, even if those reasons are not the true underlying motives (Kunda 1990). In this process of justification, they tend to selectively access a biased subset of pertinent beliefs and rules, leading them to arrive at the desired result. This rationalization process allows them to maintain a coherent self-image and defend their decisions against potential criticism or doubt.

Research by Hsee and Hastie (2006) provides further support for the idea of post-decisional rationalization. In their study, participants were asked to evaluate two different options and subsequently justify their choices. The researchers found that participants tended to generate more reasons in favor of their chosen option after making the decision. This suggests that rationalization occurs as a means of preserving a sense of consistency and confidence in decision-making.

Furthermore, fMRI studies have revealed that brain regions associated with rationalization, such as the dorsolateral prefrontal cortex (DLPFC), show increased activation during post-decisional justification processes (Sharot et al. 2011). This finding supports the notion that the rational mind becomes engaged *after* an emotional decision has been made, as individuals seek logical explanations to justify their choices.

Cognitive biases further support the idea that emotions influence decision-making. Kahneman and Tversky's prospect theory (2013) demonstrated how individuals' choices are affected by the framing of options and the emotional valence attached to potential gains and losses. This implies that emotions have the tendency to influence decision-making by either promoting risk-averse or risk-seeking behaviors.

Similarly, Loewenstein et al. (2001) demonstrated that incidental emotions, unrelated to the decision at hand, can influence choices too. Positive emotions may lead to riskier decisions, while negative emotions may result in more cautious choices.

Understanding the emotional origins of decision-making and the subsequent role of rationalization has important implications. Recognizing the influence of emotions on decision-making allows individuals to critically assess their initial emotional reactions and potentially mitigate biases. Additionally, understanding the post-decisional rationalization process can lead to improved self-awareness and help recognize when one is engaging in biased justifications. Thus, decision-making in the workplace is not a purely rational process; emotions significantly influence the choices people make.

"Have the courage to follow your heart and intuition. They somehow already know what you truly want to become. Everything else is secondary."

— Steve Jobs

Organizations and policymakers can also benefit from this knowledge by considering the emotional factors that influence decision-making. By taking into account the intricate interplay of emotions in the decision-making context, they can make more informed and effective choices that align with the needs and aspirations of individuals and communities. Understanding how emotions influence decision-making allows organizations and policymakers to design policies, strategies, and interventions that are better attuned to the underlying emotional dynamics, leading to outcomes that are not only rational but also resonate with the values and well-being of the people they serve. This recognition of emotional factors opens up new avenues for fostering positive organizational cultures, enhancing employee engagement, and driving sustainable societal change.

Emotions are contagious, and they can spread rapidly within a group or team. The phenomenon of emotional contagion can significantly influence group decision-making.

Research has shown that positive emotions, such as enthusiasm or inspiration, can enhance creativity, collaboration, and problem-solving within teams (Barsade 2002). Conversely, negative emotions, such as fear or anger, can lead to dysfunctional decision-making, reduced cooperation, and impaired problem-solving abilities (Lerner & Keltner 2000). Therefore, ignoring emotions within a team or group can have detrimental effects on the overall decision-making process and team dynamics.

Many work environments require employees to engage in emotional labor, which involves managing and regulating their emotions to meet job requirements (Hochschild 1983). The suppression or masking of emotions can lead to emotional dissonance, resulting in negative psychological and physiological outcomes for employees (Grandey 2000). Emotional dissonance and the consequent emotional exhaustion can impair decision-making abilities and increase the likelihood of errors (Hülsheger, Alberts, Feinholdt & Lang 2013). Recognizing and addressing employees' emotional well-being is essential for maintaining optimal decision-making processes in the workplace.

Fear of Authenticity and Emotional Expression in Professional Environments

In professional environments, the fear of being authentic or showing emotions is a common phenomenon that can be attributed to various factors. Understanding these factors and how they could apply to certain workplace cultures can shed light on why individuals often suppress their authentic selves and emotions in professional settings.

One primary reason individuals fear being authentic is due to the pressure to conform to societal norms and expectations. Workplaces often prioritize professionalism, which is associated with maintaining a composed and rational demeanor. This emphasis on professionalism can create a perception that displaying emotions or authenticity is a sign of weakness or unprofessionalism. Consequently, individuals may fear judgment, rejection, or being perceived as less competent if they express their true selves or show emotions.

Similarly, a fear of vulnerability is prevalent in professional settings. Many individuals perceive showing vulnerability as a risk, since it could be exploited, used against them, or seen as a sign of weakness—which, in turn, could undermine their credibility or career prospects. In highly competitive environments where success is often equated with strength and resilience, the fear of being vulnerable can be deeply ingrained.

Another factor contributing to the fear of authenticity is the hierarchical nature of many organizations. Employees may perceive that showing emotions or being authentic could challenge their position or authority within the hierarchy. They may worry about potential power imbalances, negative judgments from superiors or peers, or the loss of control over how they are perceived. This fear can hinder individuals from expressing themselves authentically and openly sharing their emotions, leading to a culture of emotional suppression.

The lack of psychological safety in the workplace is another significant factor that discourages authenticity and emotional expression. When individuals do not feel safe to express their emotions or be their authentic selves without fear of retribution or negative consequences, they are likely to suppress their emotions and adopt a more guarded persona. This fear is often fueled by a lack of trust, perceived or actual repercussions, or a history of negative experiences with emotional expression in the workplace.

Additionally, cultural and gender norms can contribute to the fear of authenticity and emotional expression. Different cultures have varying expectations regarding emotional expression in professional settings. In some cultures, there is a stronger emphasis on stoicism and emotional restraint. Gender norms may also play a role, as societal expectations may dictate that certain emotions are more acceptable for one gender than another. These cultural and gender norms can create a fear of deviating from prescribed emotional expressions, leading individuals to suppress their authentic selves.

To foster a more authentic and emotionally healthy professional environment, it is essential for organizations to prioritize psychological safety, cultivate inclusive cultures that embrace diverse emotional expressions, and provide avenues for open and honest communication. This can be achieved through leadership that role models vulnerability, encourages authentic expression, and establishes clear channels for feedback and support.

Organizations can also offer training and development programs that promote emotional intelligence, empathy, and self-awareness, empowering individuals to navigate emotions and express themselves authentically.

On another, more personal, level the most common reason why individuals fear being authentic or showing emotions in professional environments is a lack of personal values and a weak personal identity. When individuals are unsure of who they truly are, and what they stand for, they may struggle to express themselves authentically, fearing the potential consequences of revealing their true selves.

Personal values act as guiding principles that shape our behavior, decisions, and interactions with others. They reflect our core beliefs, priorities, and what we hold dear. When individuals have a strong sense of their personal values, they can confidently align their actions and emotions with those values, leading to a greater sense of authenticity. However, in the absence of clear personal values or a deep understanding of oneself, individuals may feel adrift and uncertain about their true identity and what they genuinely believe in.

In professional environments, a lack of personal values can contribute to the fear of authenticity and emotional expression. Without a strong foundation of personal values, individuals may struggle to discern how to act or respond authentically in different situations. They may fear that expressing their true emotions or beliefs could be incongruent with what is expected or accepted in the workplace, leading to potential judgment or negative consequences. This fear can lead to the suppression of emotions and the adoption of a more guarded persona, creating a disconnect between one's true self and their professional identity.

Moreover, a weak personal identity can amplify the fear of authenticity in professional settings. Personal identity is the perception and understanding of oneself as a unique individual with a distinct set of characteristics, values, and beliefs.

When individuals have a weak personal identity, they may struggle to define themselves and instead rely heavily on external validation or conforming to societal expectations. This can result in a reluctance to deviate from the norm, express emotions, or be authentic in the workplace, due to fearing damage to their professional standing through being judged, rejected, or misunderstood. This fear can create a barrier to authentic expression and lead individuals to adopt a more impersonal or detached demeanor, further perpetuating a sense of disconnection between their true selves and their professional roles. This is why many individuals often find themselves torn between what are commonly perceived as personal and professional ethics.

To overcome the fear stemming from a lack of personal values and weak personal identity, individuals must embark on a journey of self-discovery and self-awareness. This entails exploring their values, beliefs, strengths, and passions to establish a solid foundation of personal identity. Engaging in introspection, seeking personal growth opportunities, and reflecting on past experiences can help individuals gain clarity about their authentic selves and what they genuinely stand for.

Organizations also play a crucial role in fostering an environment that supports personal growth and authenticity. By creating a culture that encourages self-reflection, values individual uniqueness, and embraces diverse perspectives, organizations can empower employees to express their emotions and be true to themselves. This can be achieved through initiatives which foster open and inclusive communication channels, such as personal development programs and coaching.

The Blurred Line Between Personal and Professional Ethics

In the realm of ethical decision-making, individuals often find themselves confronted with the dilemma of distinguishing between personal ethics and professional ethics. This confusion arises from the perception that different standards apply in each domain. As a result, people may mistakenly believe that certain behaviors deemed unacceptable in their personal lives are somehow permissible or even expected in professional settings. However, it is crucial to recognize that ethics is not divided into separate compartments based on the context; rather, it is a universal principle that guides behavior and actions in all aspects of life.

Personal ethics encompasses an individual's moral principles, values, and beliefs that guide their conduct and decision-making in their personal lives. These ethics are shaped by various factors, such as upbringing, culture, religion, and personal experiences. Personal ethics act as a compass, providing guidance on how individuals should treat others, make choices, and behave in their day-to-day lives. It reflects their core principles, integrity, and commitment to doing what is right.

Professional ethics, on the other hand, refers to the ethical standards and principles that guide behavior and conduct within a specific profession or workplace. These ethics are designed to ensure integrity, fairness, and responsible behavior in professional interactions and decision-making. While they may have specific codes of conduct or guidelines tailored to the demands of a particular field, they should align with broader ethical principles.

The confusion arises when individuals fail to recognize that personal and professional ethics are not separate entities, but interconnected aspects of their moral compass. The misguided belief that different standards apply in each domain allows people to justify behaviors in professional settings that they would otherwise deem unethical in their personal lives. This misconception can lead to ethical lapses, compromised integrity, and undermined trust in professional relationships.

In reality, maintaining consistency between personal ethics and professional ethics is crucial for cultivating ethical behavior. Ethical principles are not negotiable based on context; they are rooted in fundamental notions of fairness, honesty, respect, and responsibility. Fostering strong personal ethics provides a foundation for consistently doing what is right, regardless of the setting. When personal ethics are robust, they serve as a guide, shaping behavior and decision-making in both personal and professional realms.

Ethics: A Universal Principle

Ethics, in essence, is a universal principle that transcends the boundaries of personal and professional domains. It encompasses values and principles that should guide individuals' actions and choices, regardless of the context in which they find themselves. Acting ethically means consistently upholding one's personal values and moral principles, irrespective of the situation.

When individuals deviate from their personal ethics in professional settings, the consequences can be significant. Engaging in behavior that contradicts personal values and beliefs erodes self-respect, leading to feelings of guilt, cognitive dissonance, and moral distress, which could potentially lead to serious mental health issues. Furthermore, it can strain professional relationships, damage reputations, and undermine the trust that is crucial for effective collaboration and cooperation in the workplace.

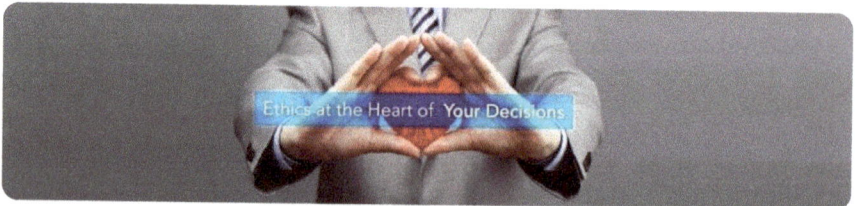
Ethics at the Heart of Your Decisions

Upholding strong personal ethics provides a foundation for consistently doing what is right, irrespective of the context. By emphasizing the importance of aligning personal and professional ethics, individuals can navigate the complexities of ethical decision-making with integrity, ensuring that ethical behavior remains a guiding force in both their personal and professional lives.

It's OK to Be Invisible: Embracing the Power of Introversion and Quiet Strength

In a world that often celebrates extroversion and outgoing personalities, the notion of being invisible may seem counterintuitive or even undesirable. Society tends to value assertiveness, charisma, and the ability to command attention. However, it is important to recognize and appreciate the unique strengths and contributions of introverted individuals who prefer a quieter, more reflective approach to life. Embracing the idea that it is okay to be invisible can lead to a deeper understanding and acceptance of introversion, fostering personal growth, meaningful connections, and a more balanced society.

Introversion is not a flaw or a weakness; rather, it is a natural personality trait characterized by a preference for solitude, deep introspection, and a lower threshold for external stimulation. Introverts derive their energy from within and often excel in introspective thinking, creativity, and focused work. They tend to listen attentively, observe keenly, and contribute thoughtfully. While extroversion is more widely celebrated, introversion brings its own set of valuable qualities to the table.

By embracing the concept of being invisible, introverts can tap into their inherent strengths and leverage them to make a significant impact. In a world that often values loud voices and visibility, introverts can offer a refreshing perspective rooted in contemplation, empathy, and deep understanding. Their ability to listen attentively and process information thoroughly can lead to insightful observations and thoughtful contributions.

Moreover, the power of introversion lies in the ability to create space for deep connections and meaningful relationships. While extroverts thrive in social settings and gain energy from external interactions, introverts cherish one-on-one connections and often prefer more intimate gatherings. By embracing their natural inclination toward solitude and introspection, introverts can foster deeper connections with others by offering their undivided attention, empathy, and thoughtful insights. It is through these quieter moments of connection that lasting bonds and authentic relationships can flourish.

Embracing invisibility also allows introverts to recharge and find solace in their own company. In a world that can be overwhelming and overstimulating, introverts often seek solitude as a means of self-care and rejuvenation. By honoring their need for quiet reflection and time alone, introverts can replenish their energy reserves and return to the world with a renewed sense of purpose and clarity.

Furthermore, the concept of being invisible challenges societal norms and encourages a more inclusive perspective. Embracing introversion as a valid and valuable way of being reminds us that not everyone thrives in the limelight or seeks constant attention. By recognizing and celebrating the strengths of introverted individuals, we can foster an environment that appreciates diverse approaches to work, communication, and problem-solving. In doing so, we create a space where everyone, regardless of their inclination toward introversion or extroversion, can thrive and contribute their unique gifts.

However, it is important to note that embracing invisibility does not mean that introverts should remain silent or hide their talents. Rather, it encourages introverts to find their voice and share their insights in a way that feels authentic and comfortable to them. It is about valuing and respecting the quieter strengths of introverted individuals, while also encouraging them to step forward when they are ready to contribute.

Adopting the idea that it is okay to be invisible can be a transformative mindset, particularly for introverted individuals. Embracing invisibility is not about shrinking away or remaining unnoticed; it is about celebrating introversion as a valid and valuable way of being. By recognizing the inherent strengths of introversion, embracing solitude, fostering meaningful connections, and challenging societal norms, introverts can harness their quiet strength and make a lasting impact, cultivating a more inclusive and balanced society. So, let us embrace the power of introversion and honor the beauty of being invisible.

Busting the Myth of Leadership and Embracing Compassion, Empathy, and Genuine Care

"One of the criticisms I've faced over the years is that I'm not aggressive enough or assertive enough, or maybe somehow, because I'm empathetic, it means I'm weak. I totally rebel against that. I refuse to believe that you cannot be both compassionate and strong."

— Jacinta Arden

In many corporate cultures, there has been a long-standing misconception about leadership, where it is often associated with harshness, coldness, and a distant demeanor. Such beliefs often stem from traditional notions of authority and power, where leaders were expected to enforce discipline, maintain control, and make tough decisions without showing vulnerability. However, this myth of leadership is rapidly being challenged as organizations recognize the immense value of compassion, empathy, and genuine care in fostering a thriving and productive work environment.

This prevailing culture of harshness and coldness has unfortunately found its way into the boardroom, creating a significant gap between board directors and the rest of the organization. This disconnect often results in an environment where fear permeates, stifling open communication and preventing valuable input from all staff.

In this traditional boardroom culture, directors may adopt an authoritative stance, distancing themselves from the rest of the organization. Their insights typically flow exclusively through interactions with the Chief Executive Officer. This can lead to a lack of understanding of the challenges faced by frontline staff and a limited perspective on customer needs and experiences. As a result, decisions may be made without fully considering the insights and expertise of those who interact directly with customers.

The consequence of this divide is twofold. First, staff—who possess valuable insights into the customer base and the intricacies of the organization's operations—may feel excluded and undervalued. Their perspectives and ideas go unheard, leading to a missed opportunity to tap into their expertise and creativity. This can be demoralizing and hinder their motivation to contribute to the organization's success.

Second, the absence of open dialogue and the fear of questioning decisions in the boardroom can result in a lack of accountability and potentially flawed decision-making. When directors are shielded from critical feedback and alternative viewpoints, the organization becomes vulnerable to blind spots and missed opportunities for improvement. It is crucial to recognize that the best decisions are often the result of collaborative and diverse input from various levels of the organization.

True leadership is far from this misconception. It is not about imposing fear or dominating subordinates; it is about inspiring and empowering individuals to unleash their full potential. Effective leaders understand that compassion and empathy are not signs of weakness, but rather strengths that fuel stronger connections, enhance trust, and promote loyalty within the team. By busting the myth of harsh leadership, organizations can cultivate an environment that encourages creativity, innovation, and collaboration, ultimately leading to sustainable success.

At the heart of true leadership is compassion. A compassionate leader recognizes the humanity in each team member, understanding that they are more than just cogs in the corporate machine. By demonstrating empathy and showing genuine concern for the well-being of employees, leaders create a sense of belonging and loyalty that drives individuals to invest their best efforts in their work. Compassionate leaders actively listen to their team members, acknowledge their feelings and perspectives, and work together to find solutions that benefit everyone involved.

Empathy is another essential aspect of true leadership. Empathetic leaders put themselves in their team's shoes, seeking to understand the challenges they face and the obstacles they encounter. This ability to empathize allows leaders to offer support, encouragement, and guidance when needed most. It creates a positive and inclusive work environment where employees feel valued, appreciated, and understood. Empathetic leaders build strong relationships with their team members, fostering a sense of trust and camaraderie that transcends the boundaries of traditional hierarchy.

Genuine care is the foundation on which compassionate and empathetic leadership is built. Leaders who genuinely care about their team and the success of the company go above and beyond to ensure that employees' needs are met, their voices are heard, and their contributions are recognized. This caring attitude is not limited to professional matters; it extends to the overall well-being of team members, recognizing the importance of work-life balance and the impact of personal challenges on performance.

Leadership that prioritizes compassion and empathy recognizes that organizations are composed of individuals, each with unique needs, motivations, and emotions. By fostering an environment where compassion and empathy thrive, leaders create a sense of psychological safety, where employees feel valued, understood, and supported. This, in turn, enhances employee well-being, engagement, and productivity.

Contrary to the myth, compassionate leadership does not imply a lack of accountability or an absence of performance expectations. In fact, compassionate leaders set clear goals and standards while also providing the necessary guidance and support for their team members to achieve those objectives. They recognize that individuals thrive when they feel empowered, encouraged, and trusted to take ownership of their work.

Furthermore, true leadership encompasses a broader perspective beyond immediate financial gains. While financial sustainability is undoubtedly important, leaders who embrace compassion and empathy understand the significance of long-term success through the cultivation of a positive corporate culture, employee well-being, and ethical practices. They consider the impact of their decisions on all stakeholders, including employees, customers, communities, and the environment.

A compassionate leader understands that employees are not merely resources to be exploited but individuals with hopes, dreams, and personal lives. They recognize that a healthy work environment is one that supports work-life integration, promotes wellness initiatives, and encourages personal and professional growth. Such leaders invest in employee development programs, mentoring, and opportunities for advancement, fostering a sense of loyalty, commitment, and engagement within the organization.

Moreover, compassionate leadership extends beyond the confines of the organization itself. Leaders who genuinely care for their teams and their company also consider their broader societal impact. They proactively engage in corporate social responsibility initiatives, promote diversity and inclusion, and advocate for sustainable and ethical business practices. By demonstrating these values, leaders inspire their teams to align their personal and professional values, contributing to a greater sense of purpose.

It is imperative to bust the myth of harshness in leadership. True leadership goes hand in hand with compassion, empathy, and genuine care for the team and the company. It is time to redefine leadership by debunking the myth and embracing a compassionate and empathetic approach that benefits both individuals and organizations alike. This can be done by confidently embracing a culture of emotional intelligence—an effective approach to addressing the gap between board directors and staff and enhancing the overall decision-making process.

Creating an Emotionally Intelligent Work Environment

To harness the positive influence of emotions on decision-making, organizations need to cultivate an emotionally intelligent work environment. This involves several key practices:

Emotionally Intelligent Leadership: Leaders should display emotional intelligence by recognizing and managing their own emotions and fostering an atmosphere that encourages open expression and understanding of emotions.

Emotionally Aware Teams: Team members should be encouraged to share their emotions and provide support to one another. Training programs and workshops can enhance emotional awareness and empathy within teams.

Emotional Regulation Skills: Employees should be equipped with emotional regulation skills to manage their emotions effectively and handle workplace challenges in a constructive manner.

Emotionally Supportive Policies: Organizations should implement policies that prioritize employee well-being, provide resources for managing stress and emotional demands, and promote a healthy work-life balance.

Organizations that recognize and embrace the importance of emotions can create an environment that fosters emotional intelligence, enhances decision-making, and promotes employee well-being. Integrating emotions into the workplace can unlock the potential for better outcomes, improved employee satisfaction, and increased overall organizational success. Hence why emotional intelligence is important in professional settings.

Chapter 2

EXPLORING THE FIVE COMPONENTS OF EMOTIONAL INTELLIGENCE

The Five Pillars of Emotional Intelligence

"Our feelings are not there to be cast out or
conquered. They're there to be engaged and
expressed with imagination and intelligence."
- T. K . Coleman

Emotional intelligence is a multifaceted concept that encompasses various components. The five key components of emotional intelligence are a crucial skill set for board directors to possess, enabling them to enhance their leadership effectiveness, navigate complex dynamics, make informed decisions in the boardroom, and foster a positive board culture.

Below is a concise overview of the five components of emotional intelligence and their significance for board directors:

Self-awareness: Self-awareness is crucial for board directors as it involves recognizing and understanding their own emotions, strengths, weaknesses, and triggers. By being self-aware, directors can effectively manage their emotions, exhibit authenticity, and make sound decisions that align with their values.

Self-regulation: Self-regulation is essential for board directors to maintain composure and control over their emotions and impulses. It enables them to navigate challenging situations with grace, adapt to changing circumstances, and act in a measured and thoughtful manner, even in high-pressure boardroom scenarios.

Motivation: Motivated board directors are driven by a strong sense of purpose and dedication to the organization's mission. They inspire their fellow directors, demonstrate enthusiasm, and encourage a high level of engagement in board discussions and decision-making processes. They exhibit dedication and resilience in pursuing board objectives and goals.

Empathy: Empathy is essential for board directors to understand and relate to the perspectives, needs, and concerns of others. By practicing empathy, directors can foster a culture of inclusivity, build trust among board members and stakeholders, and make well-informed decisions that consider the broader impact on all stakeholders.

Social skills: Board directors with strong social skills excel in communication, negotiation, and conflict resolution. They can effectively articulate their ideas, engage in constructive discussions, and build strong relationships with other directors and key stakeholders.

By exploring and developing these five components of emotional intelligence, board directors can enhance their ability to lead, contribute to a positive boardroom environment, and make well-informed decisions that drive the organization's success.

In the following sections, we will explore each component of emotional intelligence in greater detail and delve into their significance for board directors. By examining these components individually, we can gain a deeper understanding of how they contribute to effective leadership and governance in the boardroom.

Additionally, we will provide practical strategies on how board directors can enhance each of these components of emotional intelligence. By offering actionable insights, directors can proactively work towards improving each pillar of emotional intelligence, thereby strengthening their ability to lead with impact and effectiveness in the boardroom setting.

Self-Awareness and its Importance in the Boardroom

"Self-awareness is the compass that
illuminates the path to personal growth and
empowers us to navigate life's challenges with
clarity and authenticity."
— Sanela Osmic

The boardroom serves as a critical space in an organization where decisions are made and strategic planning takes place. The effectiveness and success of boardroom interactions are greatly influenced by the individuals occupying the positions of power. One key trait that plays a vital role in boardroom dynamics is self-awareness.

Self-awareness is the foundation of emotional intelligence and the key to its development as a board director. It involves recognizing and understanding one's own emotions, strengths, weaknesses, and values. When directors are self-aware, they are conscious of their thoughts, feelings, and actions. They can recognize how their emotions affect their interactions with others.

A study conducted by Day et al. (2014) emphasizes the critical role of self-awareness in leadership effectiveness. Board directors who possess self-awareness have a deeper understanding of their emotions and their impact on decision-making processes. They are better equipped to manage their reactions and maintain composure in high-pressure situations within the boardroom.

Eurich (2017) also discovered a positive relationship between self-awareness and leadership effectiveness. In the boardroom context, self-aware directors demonstrate a profound comprehension of their own areas of proficiency and areas for improvement. This self-knowledge enables them to leverage their strengths to contribute effectively to board discussions and decision-making processes.

Additionally, self-aware directors are more open to feedback and are willing to seek guidance, enhancing their ability to learn and adapt in dynamic boardroom environments. This adaptability contributes to improved board effectiveness, as self-aware directors can navigate complex challenges and make informed decisions that align with the organization's strategic goals.

Self-awareness is a critical component of effective leadership, as it allows directors to understand their leadership style, strengths, and areas for improvement. This self-awareness empowers them to lead with authenticity and make conscious efforts to enhance their effectiveness as board members.

Interestingly, research conducted by organizational psychologist Eurich (2018) reveals a significant disparity between self-perceived and actual levels of self-awareness. Surprisingly, while 95% of people believe they possess self-awareness, the reality is that only a mere 10 to 15% indeed exhibit this trait. This lack of self-awareness can have detrimental effects on their environment.

Self-awareness is closely linked to effective decision-making in the boardroom. Research by Kahneman (2011) emphasizes the importance of managing biases and cognitive limitations that can influence decision-making processes. Self-aware directors are conscious of their own biases, such as confirmation bias or overconfidence, and actively work to mitigate their impact. By recognizing their blind spots and seeking diverse perspectives, self-aware directors can make more objective and well-rounded decisions. Furthermore, self-awareness enables directors to assess their own emotional state and its potential influence on decision-making, allowing for a more balanced and rational approach.

Linking self-awareness to ethical leadership, Sosik and Megerian (2011) found that board directors who demonstrate self-awareness are more attuned to their moral compass, making them less susceptible to ethical lapses. They are more likely to act with integrity and make decisions guided by ethical principles, promoting a culture of ethical leadership.

Self-awareness contributes to building strong relationships among board directors and fostering effective communication. Boyatzis (2008) suggests that self-aware individuals are better equipped to understand and empathize with the emotions and perspectives of others through demonstration of active listening skills and open and respectful communication. By understanding their own communication style and the impact it has on others, self-aware directors can adapt their approach to create a more inclusive and collaborative boardroom environment. Strong relationships built on trust and respect enhance board dynamics, encourage diverse viewpoints, and lead to better collective decision-making.

When directors possess self-awareness, they can identify the presence of adverse emotions like frustration, anger, or impatience. This heightened awareness enables them to effectively regulate these emotions, safeguarding their relationships with others from any detrimental effects.

Effective communication is fundamental to successful boardroom interactions, and self-awareness plays a pivotal role in improving communication among board members. By being aware of their own communication style, tone, and non-verbal cues, directors can adapt their approach to suit different situations and personalities.

Possessing self-awareness also allows board members to recognize the impact of their words and actions on others, leading to more empathetic and inclusive communication. Research shows that self-awareness fosters active listening, the ability to give and receive constructive feedback, and the skill to manage conflicts effectively—

all of which contribute to inspiring trust and credibility in the boardroom.

Strategies for Developing Self-Awareness

Developing self-awareness as a board director is the first step in cultivating emotional intelligence. Here are some techniques that board directors can use:

Introspection and Self-Reflection

Introspection is a valuable tool for developing self-awareness. Taking time for self-reflection allows individuals to explore their thoughts, emotions, and actions, gaining insight into their own motivations and behaviors. Research conducted by Emmons and McCullough (2003) suggests that self-reflection promotes self-awareness, fostering personal growth and increased understanding of one's values and goals.

Engaging in activities such as journaling, meditation, or contemplative walks can facilitate introspection and help individuals gain clarity about their thoughts and feelings. It is important that directors analyze their thoughts, emotions, behavior, and response patterns on a regular basis.

Seeking Feedback and Perspective

Seeking feedback from others is an essential strategy to enhance self-awareness. Avolio and Hannah (2008) suggest that external feedback helps individuals gain a more accurate understanding of their strengths and weaknesses. Actively seeking feedback from trusted colleagues, mentors, or coaches can provide valuable insights into blind spots or areas for improvement. Being open to constructive criticism and actively listening to others' perspectives can broaden one's self-awareness and facilitate personal and professional growth. Seeking feedback from peers and subordinates can help board directors gain insights into their emotional behavior and interactions with others.

Mindfulness Practices

Mindfulness practices, such as meditation and mindfulness exercises, have been proven effective in cultivating self-awareness. Hafenbrack, Kinias, and Barsade (2014) found that mindfulness increases self-awareness by allowing individuals to observe their thoughts, emotions, and physical sensations without judgment. Regular mindfulness practice helps directors develop a non-reactive and non-judgmental stance towards their inner experiences, enabling a deeper understanding of their thoughts, emotions, and behaviors. Mindfulness also enhances self-regulation, enabling individuals to manage their emotions and reactions more effectively.

Keeping a Journal

Journaling is a powerful tool that can significantly contribute to the improvement of emotional intelligence among board directors, through providing a safe and private space for directors to explore and express their thoughts, emotions, and experiences. It encourages them to delve deeper into their own inner world, uncovering patterns, triggers, and underlying beliefs that may influence their decision-making and interactions in the boardroom. Through journaling, directors can gain valuable insights into their emotional responses, identify areas for personal growth, and develop strategies to effectively manage their emotions. This can empower board directors to make more informed decisions, cultivate empathy towards others, and foster healthier board dynamics.

Utilizing EI Assessments and Tools

Several assessments and tools can aid in developing self-awareness. Personality assessments, such as the Myers-Briggs Type Indicator (MBTI) or the Big Five Personality Model, can provide insights into one's natural tendencies and preferences.

Emotional intelligence assessments, such as the Emotional Quotient Inventory (EQ-i), measure specific emotional intelligence competencies and provide feedback on areas for development.

These assessments offer valuable insights into individual strengths, weaknesses, and areas for growth, enhancing self-awareness by providing a structured framework for self-reflection and personal development.

Creating a Supportive Network

Building a supportive network of trusted individuals can contribute to self-awareness. Surrounding oneself with individuals who encourage self-reflection, accountability, and growth through open and honest conversations is a great way to cultivate a support system for personal and professional development.

Improving self-awareness is a continuous journey that requires deliberate effort and practice, but which will result in positive personal growth, improved decision-making, enhanced emotional intelligence, and better interpersonal relationships. It empowers individuals to understand themselves more deeply, recognize their biases and limitations, and make conscious choices aligned with their values and goals. Developing self-awareness is a valuable investment, enabling directors to navigate challenges, maximize their potential, and thrive in both personal and professional domains.

Ultimately, developing self-awareness is the first step towards achieving success in emotional intelligence as a board director.

Worksheet: Self-Awareness in the Boardroom

Take some time to reflect on each question and provide thoughtful responses. Be honest with yourself as you assess your strengths and areas for improvement. Remember, self-awareness is an ongoing process, so revisit this worksheet periodically to track your progress.

Section 1: Understanding Your Emotions

1. What are the primary emotions you experience during boardroom meetings? (E.g., confidence, anxiety, frustration.)

2. How do these emotions influence your behavior, decision-making, and communication in the boardroom?

3. Are there any recurring patterns or triggers that intensify specific emotions in the boardroom? If yes, describe them briefly.

4. How effectively do you manage your emotions during challenging or high-pressure situations in the boardroom? Provide examples.

Section 2: Recognizing Your Strengths

1. Identify three emotional strengths or qualities that contribute to your effectiveness in the boardroom (e.g., empathy, resilience, adaptability).

2. How do these emotional strengths positively impact your interactions with board members, colleagues, and stakeholders?

3. Can you recall any specific situations where your emotional strengths played a crucial role in resolving conflicts or making informed decisions?

Section 3: Areas for Improvement

1. Identify three emotional challenges or areas for improvement in the boardroom (e.g., impatience, difficulty handling criticism, lack of assertiveness).

2. How do these emotional challenges hinder your effectiveness in the boardroom? Provide specific examples if possible.

3. What steps can you take to address and improve these emotional challenges? Consider practical strategies or resources that could help you develop these areas.

Section 4: Enhancing Self-Awareness

1. Reflect on a recent boardroom meeting or interaction. To what extent were you aware of your emotions, thoughts, and behaviors in that situation?

2. Did you receive any feedback or signals from others regarding your emotional expression or impact during the boardroom meeting? If yes, how did you respond to it?

3. How can you cultivate a habit of continuous self-reflection and self-monitoring to enhance your self-awareness in the boardroom? What strategies or techniques can you implement?

Self-Regulation and its Role in the Boardroom

"Until you make the unconscious conscious, it will rule your life and you will call it Fate."
— Carl Jung

In the dynamic landscape of board directorship, self-regulation plays a pivotal role in effective governance. Self-regulation entails the ability to manage and control one's emotions, impulses, and behaviors in a manner that aligns with organizational objectives and fosters healthy relationships within the boardroom.

Self-regulation involves the conscious and deliberate regulation of one's emotional responses, ensuring they are appropriate to the situation at hand. Furthermore, self-regulation is closely linked to board effectiveness. Self-regulation positively influences decision-making processes, preventing impulsive and irrational choices.

In the boardroom, self-regulated directors demonstrate the capacity to maintain composure, make rational decisions, and handle challenging circumstances without succumbing to impulsive reactions. Their ability to control their emotions allows for more objective and thoughtful decision-making, leading to better outcomes for the organization. They are adept at managing stress, displaying adaptability, and maintaining a positive influence on boardroom dynamics. This skill is essential in the boardroom, where decisions can be complex and challenging.

Ethical decision-making is a critical aspect of corporate governance. Self-regulated board directors are more likely to consider moral implications, adhere to ethical standards, and resist external pressures. By managing their impulses and emotions, self-regulated directors can make principled decisions that align with the organization's values and promote long-term sustainability.

Self-regulation plays a crucial role in managing emotions and building strong relationships in the boardroom. A study by Druskat and Wolff (2001) suggests that self-regulated individuals exhibit emotional intelligence, which positively impacts relationship-building and teamwork. In the boardroom, self-regulated directors can effectively manage conflicts, communicate assertively, and cultivate a positive and collaborative environment. Their ability to regulate emotions prevents outbursts, fosters trust, and promotes respectful interactions among board members.

"By constant self-discipline and self-control
you can develop greatness of character."
– Grenville Kleise

Self-regulation can also help directors to recognize and reduce biases, thereby improving overall decision-making in the boardroom. Bazerman, Loewenstein, and Moore (2003) emphasize the role of self-regulation in mitigating biases, claiming that self-regulated directors are better equipped to recognize and manage their own biases, such as confirmation bias or overconfidence. They are more likely to engage in critical thinking, seek diverse perspectives, and consider a range of options before making decisions, contributing to a more robust and unbiased decision-making process.

Strategies for Improving Self-Regulation

There are several strategies that board directors can employ to enhance self-regulation. Research by Lerner and Gross (2018) emphasizes the significance of self-regulation in decision-making, especially when faced with challenging or stressful conditions. In the boardroom, self-regulated directors are better equipped to manage their emotions, remain composed, and make well-considered decisions. Self-regulation also promotes ethical conduct, as it enables board directors to resist biases, conflicts of interest, and external pressures that may compromise ethical decision-making processes.

Below are some strategies board directors can use to improve self-regulation:

Develop Self-Awareness

Self-awareness is the foundation of self-regulation. Board directors should engage in introspection and reflection to gain a deep understanding of their emotions, triggers, and behavioral patterns. Regular self-assessment and feedback-seeking can provide valuable insights into areas requiring improvement.

It is important to acknowledge emotions instead of suppressing them, since recognizing and accepting emotions is the first step in managing them. Directors should also identify what triggers emotional reactions in them and the people around them. Understanding such triggers can help in better management of emotions.

Pause and Reflect

Another effective tool that can enhance self-regulation in board directors is the practice of pausing and reflecting. During moments of heightened pressure, directors should adopt the habit of pausing before providing a response. This brief moment allows them to assess their emotional state, evaluate the impact of potential responses, and choose a measured and thoughtful course of action.

Hofmann, et al. (2012) confirm the benefits of pausing and reflecting in self-regulation. By consciously creating a brief space for reflection, directors can regulate their emotions, evaluate the situation more objectively, and make decisions that are not driven solely by immediate impulses.

Additionally, pause and reflection provide directors with an opportunity to consider multiple perspectives and gather additional information before making important decisions. Research conducted by Galinsky et al. (2008) illustrates that taking time to pause and reflect allows individuals to engage in more thorough information processing. This leads to better decision outcomes and reduces the likelihood of making rash or biased judgments.

Practice Mindfulness

Mindfulness practices, such as meditation and mindful breathing exercises, have been shown to enhance self-regulation. Findings from Feruglio et al. (2022) indicate that mindfulness increases self-awareness, reduces emotional reactivity, and improves cognitive control. Engaging in regular mindfulness exercises can help board directors remain present, focused, and less reactive to stressful situations, enhancing their ability to regulate emotions.

Set Clear Goals and Priorities

Establishing clear goals and priorities helps board directors stay focused and avoid distractions. By defining their objectives, directors can allocate their time, attention, and energy more efficiently. This strategic approach to goal setting and prioritization minimizes the likelihood of impulsive decision-making and promotes thoughtful deliberation.

Time Management

Effective time management is crucial for self-regulation in the boardroom. Board directors should employ techniques such as setting realistic deadlines, creating schedules, and utilizing tools like time-blocking to optimize their productivity and avoid feeling overwhelmed. Proper time management ensures directors have sufficient time to reflect, deliberate, and make well-informed decisions.

Stress-Reduction Practices

Stress can impede self-regulation and impair decision-making abilities. Board directors should engage in stress-reduction practices such as physical exercise, relaxation techniques, or hobbies to alleviate stress and promote emotional balance. Research suggests that engaging in activities that activate the parasympathetic nervous system, such as deep breathing exercises or progressive muscle relaxation, can help regulate emotions and enhance self-control (Porges 2011).

Continuous Learning and Development

Directors should embrace a growth mindset and commit to ongoing learning and development in emotional intelligence. Engaging in professional development, attending workshops, reading relevant literature, and leveraging resources that provide insights into self-regulation techniques and best practices can improve self-regulation over time.

Improving self-regulation in the boardroom is essential for effective decision-making, ethical conduct, and positive board dynamics. Through investment in the development of self-regulation skills, directors can actively contribute to the enhancement of governance practices, thereby playing a crucial role in driving the overall success of the organization.

Worksheet: Self-Regulation in the Boardroom

Take the time to reflect on each question and provide thoughtful responses. Be honest with yourself as you assess your strengths and areas for improvement. Remember, self-regulation is a continuous process, so revisit this worksheet periodically to track your progress.

Section 1: Understanding Emotional Triggers

1. Identify three common emotional triggers or situations that evoke strong reactions from you in the boardroom (e.g., criticism, conflicts, time pressure).

2. How do these triggers typically impact your emotional state and subsequent behaviors? Provide specific examples if possible.

3. Are there any physical or behavioral signs that indicate you are becoming emotionally triggered? (E.g., increased heart rate, tensed muscles, raised voice).

Section 2: Strategies for Emotional Regulation

1. Identify three effective strategies or techniques that you currently use or could use to regulate your emotions in the boardroom (e.g., deep breathing exercises, taking a brief break, reframing perspectives).

2. Are there any additional strategies or techniques you would like to explore to enhance your emotional regulation skills? List them and briefly describe how you think they could be beneficial.

Section 3: Maintaining Professionalism and Objectivity

1. Reflect on a recent boardroom situation where you successfully demonstrated emotional self-regulation. Describe the situation briefly and explain how you managed to maintain professionalism and objectivity.

2. Recall a situation where you struggled to regulate your emotions in the boardroom. What were the consequences of that emotional outburst or lack of self-regulation?

3. Are there any specific techniques or practices you can adopt to develop a habit of stepping back, assessing situations objectively, and responding thoughtfully in the boardroom?

Section 4: Accountability and Continuous Improvement

1. Reflect on your overall progress in developing self-regulation skills in the boardroom. Have you noticed any positive changes in how you manage your emotions and behaviors? If yes, provide examples.

2. How can you hold yourself accountable for consistently maintaining emotional self-regulation in the boardroom? Are there any accountability partners or support systems you can leverage?

3. Identify one specific area or trigger that you would like to work on to further improve your self-regulation skills. Outline a plan of action with measurable steps to address this area.

The Role of Empathy in the Boardroom

"Empathy is the greatest virtue. From it, all virtues flow. Without it, all virtues are an act."
— Eric Zorn

Empathy is a vital component of emotional intelligence that plays a significant role in leadership, decision-making, and overall success in the boardroom. It involves recognizing, understanding, and relating to others' experiences, emotions, and perspectives. It is essential for effective governance and organizational success.

First and foremost, empathy enables board directors to develop a deeper understanding of the diverse stakeholders they serve, including employees, customers, investors, and the wider community. By putting themselves in the shoes of others and actively listening to their concerns and needs, directors can gain valuable insights that inform their decision-making. This empathetic understanding helps shape strategies, policies, and initiatives that align with the values and expectations of stakeholders, fostering trust, loyalty, and positive relationships.

Empathy also enhances the board's capacity to make informed and ethical decisions. By considering the potential impact of decisions on various stakeholders, directors can assess the social, environmental, and ethical implications of their choices. This empathetic perspective goes beyond pure financial considerations and contributes to sustainable governance practices that prioritize long-term value creation, corporate social responsibility, and stakeholder well-being.

In addition, empathy also plays a vital role in effective board dynamics and relationships. Directors who demonstrate empathy are more likely to build trusting and authentic relationships with their fellow board members. By understanding and appreciating each other's experiences, strengths, and challenges, directors can work together more harmoniously, leveraging their collective expertise for the benefit of the organization. Empathy facilitates effective communication, conflict resolution, and consensus-building, creating a positive and productive boardroom atmosphere.

According to Catalyst (2020), 86% of professionals with highly empathetic senior leaders and 82% with highly empathetic managers experienced greater success.

However, it is important to highlight that empathy is not sympathy. Sympathy is feeling sorry for someone, while empathy is putting yourself in someone else's shoes. Empathy requires active listening, observation, and an open mind. It involves reading non-verbal cues, such as facial expressions and body language, to understand the emotional state of others.

Empathy is crucial for effective communication. When individuals listen to others with empathy, they gain a deeper understanding of their needs, concerns, and motivations. This understanding allows them to tailor their messages to others' needs, which increases the chances of successful outcomes. It also creates a sense of trust and respect in the relationship.

Board directors are responsible for making decisions that impact the company, its employees, and its stakeholders. They need to be able to understand each other's perspectives and the perspectives of different stakeholders, then balance their interests. Empathy allows board directors to see the world through the eyes of others and make decisions that are fair and just.

Research also confirms that empathy enhances board effectiveness by promoting collaboration, understanding diverse viewpoints, and creating a sense of shared purpose (Uhl-Bien 2006). Empathetic board directors have a distinct advantage in cultivating a boardroom environment that promotes inclusivity and encourages the recognition and respect of diverse perspectives. This leads to more informed decision-making and higher levels of engagement among board members.

A study conducted by Zhu et al. (2004) emphasizes that empathetic board directors are more attuned to the needs, concerns, and aspirations of various stakeholders, including employees, customers and communities. By understanding and addressing stakeholder perspectives, empathetic directors can build trust, enhance reputation, and ensure decisions are aligned with the organization's broader impact.

Empathetic board directors are more likely to consider the moral implications and potential consequences of their decisions on different stakeholders. They take into account the human impact, ethical considerations, and social responsibility, resulting in decisions that reflect empathy and promote long-term sustainability.

Demonstrating empathy is critical in building relationships and fostering trust in the boardroom. Maddux and Galinsky (2008) suggest that empathetic individuals are more proficient in understanding and responding to the emotions and needs of others, creating a foundation of trust and cooperation. In the boardroom, empathetic directors can establish rapport, listen actively, and validate the experiences of their colleagues, creating a sense of psychological safety.

Lastly, conflict resolution is another area where empathy is essential. Disagreements and confrontations are inevitable in the boardroom; however, empathy allows directors to understand the root causes of the conflict, the emotional state of the parties involved, and the potential solutions. Board members can de-escalate conflicts and find mutually beneficial solutions by demonstrating empathy and understanding.

Cultivating Empathy in the Boardroom

Board directors should consider the following strategies to cultivate empathy:

Active Listening and Reflection

Board directors should practice active listening, which involves giving their full attention to the speaker, suspending judgment, and seeking to understand the underlying emotions and perspectives being conveyed. Reflection on conversations and experiences can also enhance empathy by allowing directors to analyze and connect with the feelings and experiences of others.

Perspective-Taking

Perspective-taking involves imagining oneself in the position of others and striving to understand their experiences and emotions. Encouraging board directors to adopt a perspective-taking mindset fosters empathy by expanding their understanding of diverse viewpoints and considering unique perspectives, needs, and challenges.

Perspective-taking has also been shown to reduce prejudice and bias, enabling directors to approach situations with a more open and empathetic mindset. Galinsky and Ku (2004) suggest that perspective-taking increases individuals' ability to recognize and appreciate diverse viewpoints, leading to more inclusive and empathetic decision-making.

Perspective-taking also enhances communication within the boardroom. When directors actively listen and strive to understand different perspectives, they create an environment that fosters open dialogue and collaborative problem-solving. Neale, Huber, and Northcraft (1987) demonstrate that perspective-taking improves the quality of decision-making by facilitating the exchange of information, encouraging diverse viewpoints, and reducing conflicts.

Cultural Competence

Gelfand et al. (2017) emphasizes the significance of cultural competence in promoting empathy and understanding across cultures. Cultural competence involves the ability to recognize, respect, and adapt to cultural differences—including norms, values, and communication styles.

To develop this skill, board directors should educate themselves about their key stakeholders' demographics, including different cultures, customs, and values, as well as strive to understand the unique challenges faced by individuals from diverse backgrounds.

Cultural competence allows directors to connect with key stakeholders on a deeper level and make decisions that consider cultural sensitivities. It also assists in creating an inclusive boardroom environment (Chen and Starosta 2000).

Research by Hofstede (1997) emphasizes the importance of cultural competence in managing cultural conflicts and ensuring effective decision-making processes, a key skill for any board director.

Emotional Intelligence Development

Other components of emotional intelligence—which include self-awareness, self-regulation, social awareness, motivation, and relationship management—are closely tied to empathy. Board directors can engage in emotional intelligence training programs and workshops to develop these skills. Emotional intelligence enables directors to recognize and manage their own emotions, as well as understand and respond to the emotions of others, enhancing their empathetic capabilities.

Experiential Learning

Experiential learning activities, such as role-playing scenarios, simulations, and case studies, can help board directors develop empathy. These activities immerse directors in situations where they can practice understanding the emotions, needs, and perspectives of stakeholders. By engaging in experiential learning, directors can gain firsthand experience in empathetic decision-making and develop a greater understanding of the human impact of their choices.

Diversity and Inclusion

Promoting diversity and inclusion within the boardroom fosters empathy by exposing directors to a range of experiences and perspectives. By ensuring diverse representation and actively seeking diverse voices, directors can expand their understanding of different stakeholder groups and increase their empathy skills.

This view is supported by Homan, et al. (2008) who suggest that diversity enhances information processing and decision-making within teams. When board directors are exposed to diverse perspectives, experiences, and backgrounds, it expands their worldview and challenges their assumptions.

Moreover, diversity and inclusion contribute to the creation of a psychologically safe boardroom environment where individuals feel comfortable expressing their opinions and concerns. Edmondson (1999) emphasizes the role of psychological safety in fostering empathy and promoting open dialogue within teams. When board directors feel psychologically safe, they are more likely to listen to and empathize with diverse viewpoints, leading to more inclusive decision-making processes.

Additionally, diversity and inclusion contribute to better decision outcomes. Page (2007) outlines that diverse groups outperform homogeneous groups in problem-solving and decision-making tasks. By embracing diversity and creating an inclusive boardroom environment, board directors gain access to a wider range of invaluable ideas, knowledge, and expertise.

Furthermore, research by Ely and Thomas (2001) highlights the importance of inclusive leadership in promoting empathy and diversity within organizations. Inclusive leaders foster a sense of belonging, encourage diverse perspectives, and actively seek input from all board directors. Their leadership style promotes empathy by valuing and appreciating the unique contributions of each director, regardless of their background or identity.

Board Evaluation and Feedback

Incorporate empathy as a part of board evaluation and seek feedback from stakeholders on the board's ability to empathize and understand their needs. This feedback loop can highlight areas for improvement and motivate directors to prioritize empathy in their governance roles.

Avoid Assumptions

Lastly, it is important that directors avoid assumptions and refrain from making judgments before understanding the emotional context. Assumptions can create barriers to understanding and hinder effective communication within the boardroom. By consciously avoiding assumptions, directors can open themselves up to truly listening and understanding the perspectives and experiences of others.

This requires actively seeking clarification, asking probing questions, and suspending judgment. By refraining from making assumptions, directors can create a safe and inclusive environment where diverse viewpoints are valued and respected, leading to improved board dynamics, more informed decision-making, and a culture of inclusivity, collaboration, and mutual respect.

In conclusion, developing empathy in the boardroom is essential for building relationships, fostering trust, and making informed and ethical decisions. By placing a high priority on empathy, board directors have the ability to foster improved governance practices and facilitate sustainable success within the organization.

Worksheet: Empathy in the Boardroom

Take the time to reflect on each question and provide thoughtful responses. Be honest with yourself as you assess your strengths and areas for improvement.

Section 1: Understanding Empathy

1. Reflect on a recent boardroom interaction where you demonstrated empathy towards a colleague, team member, or stakeholder. Describe the situation briefly and explain how you showed empathy.

Section 2: Developing Empathetic Listening Skills

1. How well do you listen to others in the boardroom? On a scale of 1-10, rate your listening skills, with 1 being poor and 10 being excellent.

2. Reflect on a recent boardroom discussion or meeting. Did you actively listen to others' perspectives and emotions? How did your listening (or lack thereof) impact the outcome or dynamics of the conversation?

3. What strategies or techniques can you implement to enhance your empathetic listening skills in the boardroom? List at least three actionable steps you can take.

Section 3: Practicing Perspective-Taking

1. Reflect on a recent boardroom situation where you encountered a disagreement or conflict. How well did you consider the perspectives and emotions of others involved?

Did you actively try to understand their point of view?

2. How can you improve your ability to take the perspective of others in the boardroom? Are there any specific techniques or approaches you can employ? Explain briefly.

3. Describe a scenario in the boardroom where you had to make a decision that affected multiple stakeholders. How did you ensure that you considered the diverse perspectives and needs of those involved?

Section 4: Fostering a Culture of Empathy

1. Assess the current level of empathy within the boardroom. Is it a supportive and empathetic environment, or is there room for improvement? Explain your observations.

2. How can you contribute to fostering a culture of empathy in the boardroom? List at least three actionable steps you can take to promote empathy among board members and colleagues.

3. Identify one specific area or challenge in which you would like to enhance your empathy skills. Outline a plan of action with measurable steps to develop empathy in that area.

Motivation and its Role in the Boardroom

Motivation is a critical aspect of emotional intelligence and can be defined as the driving force that compels individuals to take action and achieve their goals. It is crucial for effective governance because motivated directors can easily inspire and encourage others to work towards a common goal. Directors who possess high levels of motivation tend to be more resilient, focused, and better equipped to navigate challenges and setbacks.

Pink (2011) explains that intrinsic motivation arises from an individual's internal drive and desire to accomplish meaningful goals. Motivated directors provide a sense of direction and clarity, helping others feel connected to the vision and mission of the organization. Moreover, they are more likely to develop a culture of innovation, where team members feel comfortable taking risks and contributing their ideas.

Motivated board directors demonstrate the following key characteristics:

Goal orientation: Directors who are highly motivated set clear and ambitious goals, both for themselves and the organization. They strive for continuous improvement, taking initiative to pursue innovative strategies and opportunities.

Commitment: Motivated board directors are fully committed to their roles and responsibilities. They dedicate the necessary time and effort to fulfill their obligations effectively. They attend meetings prepared, actively participate in discussions, and follow through on their commitments. Their commitment is evident in their consistent engagement and willingness to go above and beyond.

Resilience: Committed directors possess a resilient mindset, allowing them to persevere through challenges and setbacks. Their determination and persistence enable them to navigate obstacles, adapt to change, and maintain focus on long-term objectives.

Proactivity: Passionate directors take initiative and demonstrate a proactive approach to their responsibilities. They actively seek out opportunities to contribute, propose new ideas, and drive positive change within the organization. Rather than waiting for issues to arise, they anticipate challenges and take preemptive action.

Strategic mindset: Enthusiastic directors possess a strategic mindset and a broad understanding of the organization's goals and challenges. They actively engage in strategic discussions, contribute valuable insights, and offer well-informed perspectives. They bring a forward-thinking approach, considering the long-term implications of decisions and seeking opportunities for growth and innovation.

Collaboration: Highly motivated board directors recognize the importance of collaboration and actively foster a culture of teamwork. They work harmoniously with other board members, leveraging their collective knowledge and expertise. They listen attentively, respect diverse opinions, and collaborate effectively to reach consensus on important matters. They understand that collaboration leads to better decision-making and outcomes.

Both motivation and emotional intelligence significantly contribute to board effectiveness. Energetic board directors with high EI are more likely to inspire and engage their colleagues, leading to increased boardroom collaboration and commitment to organizational goals. This, in turn, enhances decision-making processes and overall board performance.

Techniques for Enhancing Motivation in the Boardroom

Motivation is a crucial factor in driving boardroom effectiveness and achieving organizational success. Motivated board directors are more likely to demonstrate dedication, commitment, and enthusiasm, leading to enhanced decision-making, stakeholder engagement, and overall board performance.

Here are some techniques that can be used by board directors to enhance motivation in the boardroom:

Create a Compelling Vision

Creating a compelling vision is a powerful tool for enhancing motivation among board directors. A clear and inspiring vision serves as a guiding force that ignites passion, commitment, and a sense of purpose within the boardroom. When directors are aligned with a compelling vision, they are more motivated to work towards its realization.

A compelling vision articulates the future direction and goals of the organization in a way that resonates with directors' values and aspirations. It goes beyond mere financial targets and encompasses a broader purpose that captures the hearts and minds of the board members. By connecting their work to a larger cause, directors find deeper meaning in their roles and are driven to make a positive impact.

A captivating vision also provides a sense of direction and focus. It clarifies the board's priorities and sets the stage for strategic decision-making. Directors can align their efforts and resources towards achieving the vision, fostering a collective sense of purpose and teamwork. This shared commitment promotes collaboration, accountability, and a sense of camaraderie among board members.

Furthermore, a compelling vision instills confidence and optimism. It inspires directors to overcome challenges, persevere in the face of obstacles and seize opportunities. When directors believe in the vision, they are more willing to take calculated risks and explore innovative solutions. This proactive and resilient mindset creates an environment conducive to growth and progress.

To create a compelling vision, board directors should engage in a collaborative process that involves active dialogue, brainstorming, and consensus-building. By involving all stakeholders and considering diverse perspectives, the vision becomes inclusive and representative of the organization's values and aspirations. Regular communication and reinforcement of the vision keep it alive and at the forefront of board discussions, ensuring ongoing motivation and alignment.

Clarify Goals and Expectations

Setting clear and challenging goals for the board and individual directors provides a sense of purpose and direction. Directors should have a comprehensive understanding of their roles, responsibilities, and performance expectations. Regularly revisit and align goals with the organization's strategic objectives to maintain motivation.

Clarifying goals and expectations is a fundamental tool for improving motivation among board directors. Research conducted by Locke and Latham (2002) demonstrates the positive impact of goal setting on motivation and performance. When individuals have specific and challenging goals that are clearly communicated, it increases their commitment, effort, and persistence in achieving those goals.

Setting clear goals provides directors with a sense of direction and purpose. They can align their efforts and decisions with the desired outcomes, ensuring that their work contributes to the organization's overall strategic objectives. This alignment enhances directors' motivation as they can more easily see the direct link between their actions and the achievement of meaningful goals.

Furthermore, setting clear expectations helps directors understand the standards of performance and behavior required from them. When expectations are communicated effectively, directors have a clear roadmap for meeting and exceeding those expectations. This reduces ambiguity and promotes accountability, leading to increased motivation and a higher level of commitment.

Caza and Cameron (2008) highlight the importance of clear role expectations in enhancing motivation and job satisfaction. When board directors understand their roles and responsibilities within the governance structure, they are more likely to feel competent and motivated in carrying out their duties.

To implement this tool effectively, it is essential for boards to engage in open and transparent communication. Regular board meetings, one-on-one discussions, and written guidelines can be used to clarify goals and set clear expectations for directors. Providing feedback and recognizing achievements along the way also helps to reinforce motivation and maintain high levels of engagement.

Foster a Positive Boardroom Culture

Promote a positive and inclusive boardroom culture that values transparency, collaboration, and open communication. Encourage constructive feedback, recognition of achievements, and sharing of diverse perspectives. Celebrate successes and create opportunities for social interaction and team building.

When the boardroom environment is a positive one—characterized by trust, respect, open communication, and collaboration—directors are more likely to be motivated, engaged, and committed to their roles and organizational goals. This is supported by research undertaken by Eisenbeiss, Knippenberg, and Boerner (2008) which demonstrates the influence of positive organizational culture on employee motivation and job satisfaction. When individuals perceive their work environment as positive, it leads to higher levels of intrinsic motivation, engagement, and overall job satisfaction.

Applying this principle to the boardroom, fostering a positive culture becomes crucial for enhancing director motivation.

A positive boardroom culture promotes trust and psychological safety, enabling directors to freely express their opinions, share ideas, and engage in constructive debates. This inclusive and respectful environment encourages directors to actively contribute, collaborate, and take ownership of their responsibilities. As a result, directors feel valued, heard, and motivated to make meaningful contributions to board discussions and decision-making processes.

Furthermore, a positive boardroom culture promotes open and transparent communication. When information flows freely, directors are better informed and have a comprehensive understanding of the issues at hand. This transparency fosters trust and ensures that decisions are made based on shared knowledge and input, rather than hidden agendas or power dynamics. Such an environment motivates directors to actively participate, as they feel their contributions are respected and valued.

Nielsen et al. (2017) highlight the importance of positive leadership behaviors in shaping an optimistic organizational culture. Leaders who demonstrate supportive and empowering behaviors create an environment that fosters motivation, engagement, and commitment among employees. In the boardroom context, board chairs and senior leaders play a critical role in cultivating a positive culture by modeling respectful and inclusive behaviors.

To foster a positive boardroom culture, it is essential for boards to prioritize values such as respect, collaboration, transparency, and open communication. Regular board evaluations, training programs, and team-building activities can be employed to enhance the boardroom culture. Encouraging constructive feedback and recognizing director contributions also contribute to a positive environment that motivates directors to excel in their roles.

Provide Feedback and Evaluation

Research suggests there is positive relationship between feedback and employee motivation (Kluger and DeNisi 1996). When individuals receive specific and timely feedback about their performance, it can significantly enhance their motivation levels and subsequent performance.

Implement regular performance evaluations and provide constructive feedback to board members. Highlight areas of strength and areas for improvement, and establish action plans to support directors' growth and development.

Feedback and evaluation provide directors with valuable insights into their performance, and this self-awareness helps directors set meaningful goals and take appropriate actions to enhance their skills and contributions. When directors receive constructive feedback, it demonstrates that their work is valued and recognized, leading to increased motivation and engagement.

Furthermore, feedback and evaluation create accountability and drive continuous improvement. When directors are aware that their performance is being evaluated, they are more likely to take ownership of their responsibilities and strive for excellence.

Research conducted by Smither, London, and Reilly (2005) emphasizes the importance of feedback as a developmental tool. The study suggests that feedback, when delivered effectively, enhances individual and team performance by providing guidance and promoting self-improvement. In the boardroom context, feedback and evaluation contribute to director growth and effectiveness.

To effectively utilize feedback and evaluation as tools for improving motivation, boards should establish a structured feedback process that includes regular performance evaluations, individual coaching sessions, and opportunities for self-reflection. The feedback provided should be specific, constructive, and aligned with the board's goals and expectations.

Recognition

Recognize and appreciate directors' contributions and achievements. Acknowledging their efforts and expressing gratitude fosters a positive and motivating environment, enhancing their sense of value and satisfaction, leading to increased motivation and engagement.

O'Boyle et al. (2011) emphasize the correlation between recognition and employee motivation as a favorable one. When individuals receive recognition for their work, it has a significant impact on their motivation levels and job satisfaction. By applying this principle to the boardroom, recognition becomes a valuable tool for enhancing director motivation.

Recognition can take various forms, including verbal praise, written appreciation, awards, and public acknowledgment. When directors receive recognition for their achievements, efforts, and unique perspectives, it validates their contributions and reinforces their sense of purpose within the board. This recognition not only boosts their motivation but also fosters a positive boardroom culture where directors feel valued and appreciated.

Furthermore, recognition can be instrumental in creating a sense of camaraderie and teamwork among board directors. When directors recognize and celebrate each other's successes, it strengthens their relationships and promotes a supportive and collaborative environment. This positive dynamic further enhances motivation and encourages directors to go above and beyond in their roles.

Research has consistently highlighted the importance of social recognition in the workplace. Social recognition involves acknowledgment and appreciation from colleagues and peers. A research article by Cameron, Bright, and Caza (2004) explored the effects of social recognition on employee well-being and job performance. The study found that social recognition significantly predicted higher levels of employee self-esteem, job satisfaction, and organizational commitment. It emphasized the positive impact of social recognition on employee motivation and overall work outcomes.

Similarly, in a study conducted by Grant and Gino (2010), researchers examined the impact of social recognition on employee prosocial behavior. The study found that when employees received social recognition for their contributions, they were more likely to engage in helpful and cooperative behaviors towards colleagues. Social recognition plays a key role in promoting positive workplace behaviors and fostering a collaborative work environment, while simultaneously having a positive impact on motivation and well-being.

To effectively utilize recognition as a tool for improving motivation, boards should incorporate a culture of appreciation within their governance practices. This can take the form of regular board evaluations and feedback sessions, a structured recognition program, or establishing informal channels for expressing appreciation and celebrating director achievements.

Continuous Learning and Development

Promote a culture of continuous learning and development within the board. Encourage board members to engage in ongoing professional development opportunities, such as attending conferences or hosting in-house workshops and training programs. Learning new skills and expanding knowledge can fuel motivation and enthusiasm for their governance responsibilities.

Tannenbaum et al. (1991) suggest that when individuals receive training and development opportunities, it positively affects their motivation levels, job satisfaction, and overall performance.

Continuous learning and development enables directors to stay abreast of emerging trends, best practices, and industry advancements. It equips them with the knowledge and skills necessary to make informed decisions, contribute meaningfully to board discussions, and fulfill their governance responsibilities effectively. When directors have access to ongoing learning opportunities, they feel valued and motivated to continuously improve their expertise and contribute to the board's success.

Furthermore, continuous learning and development foster a growth mindset among directors. By encouraging a culture of learning and providing opportunities for professional development, boards create an environment that values curiosity, innovation, and intellectual growth. This, in turn, enhances directors' motivation, as they are encouraged to explore new ideas, challenge assumptions, and seek continuous improvement in their roles.

Likewise, findings from Day, Harrison, and Halpin (2009) emphasize the importance of leadership development programs in promoting motivation and engagement. The study suggests that leadership development interventions positively impact leaders' self-awareness, self-efficacy, and motivation. In the boardroom context, providing development programs specific to directors' needs can enhance their leadership skills and motivation to contribute effectively.

To implement continuous learning and development as tools for improving motivation, boards should prioritize professional development programs, training workshops, conferences, and access to relevant resources. Tailoring development opportunities to address directors' specific needs and interests fosters a sense of investment in their growth and competence. Regular evaluation and feedback on development initiatives also plays a crucial role in enhancing motivation and ensuring that directors' learning objectives are being met.

Through the application of these strategies, directors can amplify their emotional intelligence, motivation, and determination. Active participation from enthusiastic board members is essential to good governance and achieving the desired outcomes.

Worksheet: Motivation in the Boardroom

Take the time to reflect on each question and provide thoughtful responses. Be honest with yourself as you assess your strengths and areas for improvement.

Section 1: Understanding Your Motivations

1. What motivates you to excel in your role within the boardroom? Identify three key factors or values that drive your performance (e.g., personal growth, making a positive impact, financial success).

2. How do these motivations align with the goals and objectives of the boardroom and the organization as a whole?

3. Reflect on a recent achievement or success in the boardroom. What motivated you to pursue that goal, and how did it impact your performance?

Section 2: Setting Meaningful Goals

1. Describe a specific goal you have set for yourself in the boardroom. Is it aligned with your personal motivations and the overall vision of the organization?

2. How do you break down and prioritize your goals into smaller, actionable steps? Explain your approach.

3. Reflect on a time when you faced a significant challenge or setback in the boardroom. How did you stay motivated and bounce back from that setback? What strategies did you employ?

Section 3: Fostering Motivation in Others

1. How do you inspire and motivate your colleagues, team members, or stakeholders in the boardroom? Provide specific examples of actions or behaviors you engage in to promote motivation.

2. Are there any strategies or techniques you could incorporate to enhance your ability to motivate and empower others in the boardroom?

3. Reflect on a time when you successfully influenced a team or group of individuals to achieve a shared goal in the boardroom. What motivational strategies did you employ, and what was the outcome?

Section 4: Cultivating a Motivational Environment

1. Reflect on the overall atmosphere and culture in the boardroom. Does it foster motivation, collaboration, and a sense of purpose? If not, what changes or improvements could be made?

2. How can you contribute to creating a motivational environment in the boardroom? List specific actions or behaviors you can adopt or promote.

3. Identify one area or aspect of your own motivation that you would like to strengthen. Outline a plan of action with measurable steps to enhance your motivation in that area.

Emotional Intelligence in Boardroom Relationships

Emotional intelligence plays a critical role in cultivating effective relationships within the boardroom. Boardroom relationships involve complex dynamics and interactions among directors, and emotional intelligence helps navigate these dynamics with understanding and empathy. The ability to understand and manage one's own emotions, as well as recognize and respond to the emotions of others, can make all the difference in achieving a productive and harmonious boardroom environment.

Building Trust and Rapport with Other Board Directors

Building trust and rapport with other board directors is a critical aspect of effective boardroom dynamics and collaboration. Trust forms the foundation for productive relationships, open communication, and successful decision-making. Establishing strong connections among board directors fosters an environment of mutual respect, enhances teamwork, and ultimately contributes to the overall effectiveness of the board.

Daniel Goleman (1998) highlights the importance of emotional intelligence in leadership and decision-making. In the boardroom, where diverse perspectives and high-stakes decisions prevail, emotional intelligence plays a critical role in fostering positive relationships and effective governance.

Trust is the new currency of business and a cornerstone of effective boardroom relationships. Emotional intelligence is a key factor in building and maintaining trust, therefore directors with high EI who are more attuned to the emotions and needs of others are well-placed to do this.

The first step in building trust with other board members is to demonstrate respect for and genuine interest in their contributions, concerns, and perspectives. It is essential not to interrupt or dismiss their thoughts, but instead ask clarifying questions and make an effort to comprehend their perspective.

Consistency and reliability are crucial for building trust and establishing rapport. By consistently following through on commitments and meeting deadlines, one demonstrates accountability and takes responsibility for their actions, including any mistakes or missteps. This dedication to the board and commitment to collaborative work with other directors strengthens trust and fosters a positive working relationship.

Building strong relationships with other board directors also requires empathy and the ability to recognize and respond appropriately to their emotions. This involves being attuned to non-verbal cues, such as facial expressions and body language, and responding empathetically to the emotions that are being conveyed. For example, if a board member is expressing frustration or disappointment, acknowledging their feelings and offering support can help to build trust and rapport.

Effective boardroom relationships are characterized by collaboration and teamwork, in which emotional intelligence plays a critical role (Urch-Druskat and Wolff 2001). Trust and rapport within the boardroom are not built overnight. It requires ongoing effort and investment.

Respectful disagreement in the boardroom creates an environment where healthy debates and diverse viewpoints can thrive. While it is crucial to encourage the expression of different ideas, conflicts should always be handled in a professional manner. When directors respectfully disagree, it opens the door to better decision-making and more efficient solutions.

In the boardroom, it imperative to make an intentional effort to establish personal connections with each individual. Taking the time to sincerely get to know fellow board members on a personal level fosters a sense of camaraderie and understanding. Through genuine authenticity and openness, board members can create an atmosphere of trust and collaboration, enabling more impactful teamwork and decision-making. Investing in personal connections goes beyond titles and roles, promoting empathy and respect for one another's unique perspectives and experiences.

Finally, it is important to be open and transparent in communication with others. It is crucial to avoid hidden agendas or the withholding of information that may affect the board's decision-making process. Instead, directors should aim to foster an environment of open and honest information sharing, and be willing to engage in respectful debates and discussions.

These practices, driven by emotional intelligence, foster trust and rapport among directors, creating a solid foundation for effective governance and decision-making.

Understanding the Emotions of Board Directors and Responding Accordingly

As a board director, it is important to recognize the role emotions play in shaping the dynamics of boardroom relationships. By cultivating emotional intelligence, directors can navigate and respond to the emotional landscape within the boardroom, promoting understanding, empathy, and effective communication. This enables them to build strong and productive relationships with their peers, contributing to a harmonious and collaborative board environment.

First and foremost, it is important to recognize that board directors are human beings who are susceptible to a range of emotions. Thus, it is not uncommon for directors to experience feelings of anxiety or even anger during board meetings. These emotions may stem from a variety of factors, including differing opinions on important issues, concerns about the organization's performance, or personal conflicts with other board directors.

It is important to respond to these emotions in a way that is both empathetic and productive. This means actively listening to the concerns of fellow directors, acknowledging their emotions, and working to find common ground. It also means avoiding personal attacks or dismissive responses, which can escalate tensions and damage relationships.

One key strategy for managing emotions in the boardroom is to focus on shared goals and objectives. By reminding directors of the organization's mission and vision, it is possible to shift the focus away from personal conflicts and towards achieving common goals.

This can help to build a sense of unity and shared purpose among directors, which can in turn lead to more productive and effective decision-making.

An additional critical aspect of emotional intelligence in the boardroom is the ability to recognize and respond to non-verbal cues. These cues encompass a wide range of communication signals, including facial expressions, body language, tone of voice, and choice of words. By attentively observing and interpreting these cues, directors can gain deeper insights into the emotions and underlying dynamics within the boardroom, and respond accordingly.

Emotional intelligence is a critical skill for building successful boardroom relationships. Recognizing and responding to the emotions of their colleagues in a productive and empathetic way helps directors create a more positive and effective boardroom environment.

Conflict Management and Resolution

Conflict is an inevitable part of boardroom dynamics, often arising from differing perspectives, goals, and priorities. However, effective conflict management and resolution are essential for building successful boardroom relationships. Emotional intelligence plays a significant role in navigating these situations and finding solutions that benefit everyone involved.

Salovey and Mayer (1990) introduced the concept of emotional intelligence and emphasized its role in interpersonal relationships. In the boardroom, conflicts can be detrimental to decision-making processes, relationships, and overall board effectiveness. Emotional intelligence equips board members with the skills necessary to manage conflicts in a constructive and productive manner. It promotes understanding and empathy, crucial components in resolving conflicts in the boardroom.

When confronted with conflict, it is crucial to understand the underlying motivations of each side involved. Empathy is indispensable in achieving this understanding. By putting oneself in the shoes of others and endeavoring to perceive the world from their perspective, one can gain valuable insights into their desires and concerns. This empathetic approach enables a director to identify common ground and collaborate on finding a solution that benefits all parties involved.

Neglecting to address disagreements and conflicts within the boardroom in a timely and effective manner can have detrimental consequences that impact a company's operations and performance. If these issues are left unattended, they have the potential to escalate into acrimonious and public disputes, leading to significant and enduring repercussions for the organization and its stakeholders. Such disputes can lead to poor performance, instill fear among investors, result in resource wastage, divert valuable resources, decrease share values, and in extreme cases, bring a company to a standstill.

According to the Centre for Effective Dispute Resolution (2019), nearly one-third (precisely 29.6%) of board directors reported firsthand experience with a boardroom dispute that had significant implications for the survival of an organization. Organizations must address and resolve these conflicts promptly to mitigate the negative impacts and safeguard the overall health and stability of the company.

Effective communication stands as another vital element in conflict management and resolution. Being emotionally intelligent means being in tune with and able to articulate one's own feelings and those of others around them. When conflicts arise, it is important to listen actively, express oneself clearly and respectfully, and seek feedback to ensure that everyone is on the same page. Directors may establish the mutual respect and trust necessary for productive board meetings by improving their communication skills.

It is also important to approach conflicts with an open mind and a willingness to compromise. Emotionally intelligent directors are flexible and adaptable. Strong convictions and principles are essential, but so is the humility to acknowledge that others may be right. Directors can discover innovative solutions that benefit all parties involved by being open to different ideas and perspectives.

Last but not least, it is important to approach conflict management with a positive attitude. Maintaining composure under pressure is a hallmark of emotional maturity. The atmosphere within the boardroom can be enhanced when directors maintain an optimistic mindset and collaborate in seeking solutions.

Developing effective conflict management and resolution skills is crucial for fostering successful relationships within the boardroom. Directors can effectively navigate conflicts and identify mutually beneficial solutions by applying principles of emotional intelligence, including empathy, effective communication, flexibility, and positivity.

Effective Communication and Active Listening

Effective communication and active listening are critical skills for success in any business environment, and they hold even greater significance within the boardroom. The boardroom serves as the central hub where critical decisions are made, strategies are formulated, and company goals are set. To ensure the smooth functioning of the boardroom and maximize its potential, effective communication and active listening must be embraced.

Directors must be able to communicate effectively with their peers, stakeholders, and the public. Effective communication requires active listening, which is about more than just hearing the words being spoken. It is the ability to listen attentively and respond appropriately to the message being conveyed, and involves paying attention to the tone, body language, and other non-verbal cues that accompany the message. This is important because non-verbal cues can convey information that words cannot. For example, a person's tone of voice can indicate whether they are being sincere or sarcastic.

To be an effective listener, directors must also be present in the moment. This means giving their full attention to the speaker and avoiding distractions such as phones or other devices. It also means being open-minded and receptive to the speaker's message, even if they may not agree with it.

Effective communication also requires clarity in one's own message. It is important to be clear and concise in communication to avoid confusion or misunderstandings. This can be achieved by using simple language and avoiding technical jargon or acronyms that may not be familiar to everyone.

Due to the intensity of feelings that frequently arise during discussions on weighty topics, emotional intelligence is a key component of both successful communication and attentive listening. Directors can cultivate their emotional intelligence by acknowledging and effectively regulating their own emotions, allowing them to avoid impulsive emotional reactions and respond in a composed and logical manner.

Emotionally intelligent directors have a better grasp of the nuances of active listening and can more effectively build trust and rapport with their colleagues due to this skill. Hence, the keys to creating strong connections in the boardroom are clear communication and attentive listening.

Worksheet: Relationship Management in the Boardroom

Take the time to reflect on each question and provide thoughtful responses. Be honest with yourself as you assess your strengths and areas for improvement.

Section 1: Building Positive Relationships

1. Reflect on your current relationships with board members, colleagues, and stakeholders. How would you describe the overall quality of these relationships? Are there any areas that require improvement?

2. Identify three strategies or approaches you currently use or could use to build and strengthen positive relationships in the boardroom (e.g., active listening, seeking feedback, demonstrating appreciation).

Section 2: Effective Communication

1. How well do you communicate with others in the boardroom? On a scale of 1-10, rate your communication skills, with 1 being poor and 10 being excellent.

2. Reflect on a recent boardroom interaction or meeting. Did you effectively communicate your thoughts, ideas, and emotions? How did your communication style impact the outcome or dynamics of the conversation?

3. What strategies or techniques can you implement to enhance your communication skills in the boardroom? List at least

three actionable steps you can take.

Section 3: Conflict Resolution

1. Reflect on a recent conflict or disagreement that arose in the boardroom. How did you handle the situation? Were you able to resolve the conflict effectively? If not, what could you have done differently?

2. How comfortable are you at managing conflicts and disagreements in the boardroom? Identify any areas of improvement or specific challenges you face.

3. What steps can you take to enhance your conflict resolution skills in the boardroom? Consider strategies such as active listening, empathy, and finding win-win solutions.

Section 4: Influencing and Collaboration

1. Reflect on a recent decision-making process in the boardroom where you successfully influenced others to support your perspective or idea. Describe the situation briefly and explain the strategies you used.

2. How well do you collaborate with others in the boardroom? On a scale of 1-10, rate your collaboration skills, with 1 being poor and 10 being excellent.

3. Identify one specific area or challenge in which you would like to enhance your relationship management skills. Outline a plan of action with measurable steps to develop your skills in that area.

Making Sound Decisions with Emotional Context

The ability to make sound decisions in the boardroom is vital for the success of any organization. Decision-making is a complex process that involves evaluating various factors, including data, opinions, and potential consequences. It is a process of choosing the best course of action from several available alternatives for solving a problem or achieving a goal.

Effective decision-making is vital for organizational success because it enables directors to make informed decisions that support growth and innovation. Emotional intelligence plays a significant role in enhancing decision-making processes by integrating rational analysis with emotional awareness and management.

Emotions are part of decision-making and choices are not founded on reasonable and logical reasoning only. Lerner, et al. (2015), amongst others, recognizes the influence of emotions on decision-making. Emotions can impact cognitive processes, bias judgments, and affect the evaluation of options. Emotionally intelligent directors can recognize and manage their emotions, use empathy to understand others' perspectives and emotions, and apply these insights to solve problems effectively. This awareness and understanding of emotions enable directors to make more informed and balanced decisions.

One aspect of emotional intelligence critical to making sound decisions is self-awareness. According to Szczygiel and Mikolajczak (2017) self-awareness is positively correlated with decision-making effectiveness. Board directors who possess self-awareness can accurately assess their own strengths, weaknesses, biases, and values, enabling them to make decisions that align with their personal and organizational goals.

Furthermore, emotional intelligence enhances the ability to consider the perspectives and emotions of others, promoting inclusive decision-making. Ashkanasy and Daus (2002) stress the importance of empathy, another component of emotional intelligence, in decision-making processes. Board directors who can empathize with the concerns and emotions of stakeholders are more likely to make decisions that take into account the diverse needs and perspectives of those affected by the decision.

Emotional intelligence also aids in managing conflicts and navigating challenging decision-making situations. This has been supported by Druskat and Wolff (2001) who identified the role of emotional intelligence in facilitating constructive team dynamics during decision-making processes. Board directors who are skilled in emotional intelligence can effectively manage conflicts, build consensus, and leverage the collective wisdom of the board to make well-informed decisions.

Moreover, emotional intelligence helps board directors recognize and manage biases that can hinder sound decision-making. Emotional intelligence can mitigate the impact of cognitive biases, such as confirmation bias or anchoring bias, that may distort judgment and decision-making. Directors who possess emotional intelligence are also better equipped to identify and challenge their own biases, leading to more objective and rational decision outcomes.

In conclusion, directors with high emotional intelligence can balance rational thinking and emotional context to make sound decisions that boost organizational success.

Strategies for Improving Decision-Making

Improving decision-making in the boardroom is crucial for effective governance and organizational success. Below are several strategies that board directors can employ to enhance the decision-making process within the boardroom context:

Develop and implement decision-making frameworks: Establish clear decision-making frameworks or processes that outline how decisions will be made. This can include defining decision criteria, evaluating alternatives, considering emotional context, and making the final decision.

Create a diverse team: A diverse team can bring different perspectives, experiences, and information to the table, leading to better decision-making.

Foster an open and transparent culture: An open and transparent culture allows directors to share their opinions and ideas without fear of retribution. It leads to better collaboration and decision-making.

Encourage dialogue: Promote open and honest dialogue among directors, executives, stakeholders, and customers. This can lead to better-informed decisions as a result of taking a wide range of views into account.

Emphasize long-term perspective: Encourage board members to consider the long-term implications of their decisions. This involves assessing potential risks, evaluating sustainability aspects, and aligning decisions with the organization's long-term goals.

Seek external expertise: Consider bringing in external experts or consultants who can provide specialized knowledge and insights on specific issues or industries. Their expertise can supplement the board's decision-making capabilities.

Evaluate decision outcomes: Regularly evaluate the outcomes of board decisions to identify areas for improvement. This feedback loop can help refine the decision-making process and assist with making more informed choices in the future.

Coaching and mentoring: Seek out mentors or coaches who can assist in enhancing the decision-making abilities of individual board members and the board as a whole. They can provide feedback, support, and best practices for better decision-making processes.

Consciously and deliberately, board members may improve the quality of boardroom decision-making processes and dynamics by applying these practices, leading to more well-informed, and consequential boardroom decisions.

Effective decision-making in the boardroom brings multiple benefits, such as:

- Improved organizational performance

- Higher levels of trust and credibility from stakeholders
- Increased innovation and agility
- Better reputation among investors and customers
- Reduced risk and efficient management of resources
- More avenues for growth and expansion.

Effective decision-making involves balancing rational thinking with emotional context to make sound decisions. By incorporating the aforementioned techniques into their decision-making process, directors can enhance their ability to make informed decisions, provide relevant recommendations, and ultimately improve organizational performance and success.

Developing Emotional Intelligence in Board Directors

Emotional intelligence is a critical skill that every board director should possess. The role of emotional intelligence in building successful boardroom relationships cannot be overstated. Board members who possess emotional intelligence are better equipped to effectively manage their emotions, establish strong relationships, and communicate efficiently with fellow board members and stakeholders.

Developing emotional intelligence requires a commitment to personal growth and self-awareness. It involves understanding one's own emotions and the emotions of others, and using this knowledge to make informed decisions and build strong relationships. Emotional intelligence is not an innate trait, but rather one that can be cultivated through learning and experience.

To develop emotional intelligence as a board director, it is essential to start by understanding one's own emotional triggers and patterns. This can be achieved through self-reflection, meditation, or working with a coach or mentor who can help identify blind spots and suggest improvement.

Developing emotional intelligence also requires forging solid bonds with other board members. This involves active listening, empathy, and a willingness to understand and support the perspectives of others. Those on the board who are emotionally intelligent are more adept at handling disputes, finding common ground, and building consensus.

To be emotionally intelligent in the boardroom, one must also be able to communicate effectively. Directors with strong communication skills can better convey complex information, listen actively, and have fruitful discussions with their peers. This can help build trust and collaboration, leading to more successful outcomes and stronger relationships with stakeholders.

Directors need to have high levels of emotional intelligence to be able to read and comprehend the emotions of their peers, cultivate trust and rapport, manage conflicts effectively, create a positive boardroom culture, and lead by example. By elevating their emotional intelligence, directors have the opportunity to enhance both their personal effectiveness and the effectiveness of the organizations they lead.

Chapter 3

EMOTIONAL INTELLIGENCE
IN ACTION

Emotional Intelligence in Times of Crisis and Change

Emotional intelligence in action within a boardroom is a powerful catalyst for effective governance and decision-making. Directors who possess high emotional intelligence are adept at recognizing and managing their own emotions, as well as understanding the emotions of others. They cultivate self-awareness, allowing them to make sound decisions even in high-pressure situations.

In today's fast-paced and unpredictable business landscape, organizations frequently face crises and significant periods of change. During such times, the role of emotional intelligence becomes paramount for board directors.

Research indicates that emotional intelligence plays a vital role in effective crisis management. According to a study by Druskat and Wolff (2001), emotionally intelligent leaders are better equipped to handle the intense emotional demands of crisis situations. They exhibit composure and adaptability, maintaining a sense of calm amidst chaos and serving as anchors, inspiring confidence in others. A study by Coutu (2002) also reveals that emotionally intelligent leaders demonstrate empathy towards employees, fostering a supportive environment and enabling effective communication during crises.

Moreover, emotional intelligence enables directors to make sound decisions during times of crisis. Research by Druskat, Mount, and Sala (2006) suggests that emotional intelligence positively correlates with effective decision-making under pressure. Emotionally intelligent leaders are adept at considering both rational and emotional factors, avoiding hasty or irrational judgments. They are skilled at managing their biases and can objectively assess risks and opportunities, leading to more informed and strategic decisions that safeguard the organization's interests.

During periods of significant change, emotional intelligence is critical in the boardroom. Emotionally intelligent directors are better equipped to handle the emotional roller coaster that accompanies change. They possess the self-awareness necessary to understand their own reactions and biases, allowing them to adapt and lead with confidence. Emotionally intelligent directors can also communicate change effectively, inspiring and motivating their teams to embrace new initiatives and directions.

Furthermore, emotional intelligence facilitates effective change management. A study by Cherniss and Adler (2000) reveals that emotionally intelligent leaders foster trust and build strong relationships with their teams, resulting in greater acceptance and engagement during times of change. They actively listen to concerns, empathize with teams' emotions, and address their needs, minimizing resistance and fostering a collaborative environment.

Emotional intelligence also contributes to the development of resilience within organizations undergoing change. Research by Ashkanasy and Daus (2005) highlights that emotionally intelligent leaders create a psychologically safe environment where employees feel comfortable expressing their emotions and ideas. This fosters a culture of open communication, adaptability, and innovation, enabling organizations to navigate change with agility and resilience.

> "If you judge people, you have
> no time to love them."
> — Mother Teresa

Emotional intelligence empowers directors to manage their own emotions and empathize with others, fostering a sense of understanding and support. By recognizing and regulating their emotions, board directors can make well-informed decisions in the face of uncertainty and ambiguity. This helps create a sense of stability and confidence not just within the boardroom but also permeating throughout the entire organization.

EI also helps directors engage with stakeholders effectively during times of crisis and change. Directors who understand and address the emotional needs and concerns of stakeholders can effectively communicate with empathy, offer support, and uphold transparency. This helps build trust, foster loyalty, and navigate through challenges while preserving stakeholder relationships.

Research consistently highlights the positive impact of emotional intelligence in crisis management, decision-making, change communication, and fostering resilience within organizations. To drive sustainable success, it is imperative that directors prioritize the development and application of emotional intelligence in the boardroom, equipping themselves with the skills necessary to lead organizations through challenging times.

Assessing the Emotional Intelligence of the Board

As expressed by Daniel Goleman (2015):

> The most effective leaders are all alike in one crucial way: they all have a high degree of what has come to be known as emotional intelligence. It's not that IQ and technical skills are irrelevant. They do matter, but they are the entry-level requirements for executive positions. My research and other recent studies clearly show that emotional intelligence is the *sine qua non* of leadership. Without it, a person can have the best training in the world, an incisive, analytical mind, and an endless supply of smart ideas, but he still won't make a great leader.

While 89% of C-suite executives excel in left-brain functions, 65% conceded that their right brain was not entirely engaged, according to the findings of a study conducted by Korn Ferry (n.d.). In simpler terms, this implies that although they may possess business acumen and financial expertise, these senior professionals recognize a deficiency in right-brain-oriented abilities such as empathy and self-regulation. After all, these elements are crucial aspects of emotional intelligence, highlighting an area of improvement for these leaders.

"If you find yourself saying, 'But I am just being honest,' chances are you have just been unkind. Honesty does not heal. Empathy does."
— Dan Waldschmidt

Assessing board emotional intelligence requires a comprehensive approach considering both individual and group dynamics. So far, research or studies that exclusively measure emotional intelligence in the boardroom are pretty limited. When they are proactive in assessing and understanding emotional intelligence, boards can identify areas for improvement and implement strategies to enhance their collective emotional intelligence, fostering a boardroom environment that drives effective decision-making and organizational success.

Druskat and Wolff (2001) indicate that a group, "...must attend to yet another level of awareness and regulation. It must be mindful of the emotions of its members, its own group emotions or moods, and the emotions of other groups and individuals outside its boundaries."

For boards, evaluating group emotional intelligence means actively assessing and cultivating a board culture that promotes emotional awareness, empathy and effective emotional regulation. By recognizing and understanding the emotions of individual board members, the board as a whole can foster a supportive and collaborative environment.

Being attuned to the impact of collective emotions or moods within the board allows for timely interventions and adjustments to maintain a positive and productive atmosphere during board discussions and decision-making processes.

Boards should also be mindful of how their emotions and interactions impact other groups and individuals outside their boundaries. This requires considering the emotional implications of board decisions and actions on stakeholders, such as shareholders, employees, and the wider community.

Exploring the Levels of Group Emotional Intelligence

Boards need to build emotional capacity and influence emotions on three levels:

1. Working with individuals' emotions
2. Regulating individuals' emotions
3. Working with group emotions.

Individual emotional intelligence involves awareness and regulation of one's own and others' emotions. Group emotional intelligence adds awareness and regulation of team members', group, and external emotions. Dysfunctions can arise when emotional incompetence exists at any level. Establishing group norms promoting awareness and emotion regulation at these three levels can lead to better outcomes.

Working with individuals' emotions: To work with individuals' emotions, boards should be emotionally intelligent towards members who have different perspectives. This entails being aware of and understanding challenges that arise, such as recognizing defensive behaviors or variances in perspectives.

Regulating individuals' emotions: Regulating individuals' emotions involves positively impacting how emotions are expressed and how board members feel. Facilitating open discussions and showcasing caring behaviors can help regulate emotions and maintain trust within the boardroom.

Working with group emotions: Working with group emotions involves being aware of emotions at the group level. Self-evaluation and soliciting feedback from others can increase group emotional awareness. Building emotional capacity and creating affirmative environments are crucial for regulating group emotions. Proactive problem-solving and considering cross-boundary relationships contribute to emotional intelligence outside the group.

Measuring Individual Emotional Intelligence

Board members and executive teams work together to achieve goals via strategic planning and teamwork. Assessing the emotional intelligence of board members through standard tests may provide some insights into their capacities in handling interpersonal dynamics, facilitating communication, and creating a cohesive and productive team environment. Listed below are some tools that can be employed to evaluate individual EI.

- **EQ-i 2.0® and EQ 360® Emotional Intelligence Assessment for Leadership from Myers-Briggs:** These assessments focus on evaluating emotional intelligence in leadership roles. They provide insights into various dimensions of emotional intelligence, such as self-awareness, self-regulation, empathy, and social skills. The EQ 360® version also gathers feedback from colleagues, providing a more comprehensive understanding of an individual's emotional intelligence.

- **MindTools:** MindTools offers a range of emotional intelligence assessments and resources. Their assessments help individuals identify their emotional strengths and areas for development, providing guidance on improving emotional intelligence skills.

- **Institute for Health and Human Potential:** The Institute for Health and Human Potential offers various emotional intelligence assessments, including the Emotional Quotient Inventory (EQ-i), in which different aspects of emotional intelligence are measured, such as emotional self-awareness, assertiveness, empathy, and stress tolerance.

- **Mayer-Salovey-Caruso Emotional Intelligence Test (MSCEIT, V 2.0):** Developed by leading researchers in emotional intelligence, this test assesses the ability to perceive, use, understand, and manage emotions. It evaluates different aspects of emotional intelligence, including perception, facilitation, understanding, and management.

- **Self-Assessment:** There are some challenges in the self-assessment of emotional intelligence. A leader's self-assessment of their behavior and skills often does not align with assessments made by others. Previous research suggests that behavioral measures of emotional intelligence (such as 360-degree assessments) might have a stronger and more consistent relationship with life and work outcomes than self-assessment measures.

Recognizing Emotional Intelligence in the Boardroom

Although there is no standard method of identification, there are several indicators that a board as a whole displays high levels of emotional intelligence.

High EI boards foster a sense of purpose among members, promoting active engagement and creative tension within a framework of teamwork and respect for diverse viewpoints. These boards also exhibit learning agility, enabling them to swiftly adapt to the rapid pace of technological and societal changes.

One way to identify emotional intelligence in board directors is through careful observation of their behaviors and interactions. Emotionally intelligent individuals often exhibit self-awareness, empathy, and effective communication skills. They demonstrate the ability to manage their own emotions and understand the emotions of others, fostering positive relationships and creating a supportive boardroom environment.

Goleman et al. (2013) outlines the importance of observing non-verbal cues—such as facial expressions, body language, and tone of voice—to gauge emotional intelligence. These cues can provide valuable insights into directors' ability to understand and regulate their emotions, as well as their sensitivity to others' emotions.

Here are some benefits of emotionally intelligent boards:

Open and inclusive communication: Emotionally intelligent boards cultivate a secure environment where diverse perspectives are encouraged and respected, thereby promoting frank and open communication.

Respecting the diversity of viewpoints: Recognizing the value of differing viewpoints for improved decision-making, the board approaches conflicts with respect, concentrating on finding solutions rather than making personal assaults.

Empathy and understanding: Board members might display genuine concern and support for others, taking their emotions, needs, and concerns into account and establishing relationships based on trust and mutual regard.

Emotional self-awareness: Board members are aware of their own emotions, biases, and impact on others, assuming responsibility for effectively managing them during discussions and decision-making.

Collaborative decision-making: The board values participation, seeks diverse perspectives and expertise, and makes decisions collectively by utilizing all members' intelligence and emotional insights.

Adaptability and resilience: Board members maintain composure and resilience in the face of adversity, displaying emotional stability and the capacity to navigate complex issues while embracing learning and personal development.

Focusing on stakeholders' interests: The board prioritizes the needs and interests of stakeholders, considering the affective impact of decisions on employees, customers, shareholders, and the community at large.

Ethical decision-making: Above anything else, the board members uphold integrity, transparency, and impartiality, taking into account the ethical repercussions of decisions.

By attentively observing these behaviors and qualities in board members, valuable insights can be obtained regarding their emotional intelligence levels and the subsequent impact on effective leadership and boardroom dynamics.

Worksheet: Group Emotional Intelligence in the Boardroom

Take the time to reflect on each question and provide thoughtful responses. Discuss these questions with your board members and encourage open and honest discussions.

Section 1: Awareness of Emotions

1. How well does your board collectively demonstrate awareness of their own emotions and the emotions of others during discussions and decision-making processes? Rate the group's level of awareness on a scale of 1-10, with 1 being low and 10 being high.

2. Reflect on recent boardroom meetings or interactions. Were there instances where board members effectively recognized and acknowledged the emotions and reactions of others? Provide specific examples.

3. Are there any specific challenges or areas where the group could improve their awareness of emotions? If yes, describe these challenges and discuss potential strategies for improvement.

Section 2: Emotional Regulation

1. How effectively does the group collectively regulate their emotions during boardroom discussions and decision-making? Rate the group's ability to regulate emotions on a scale of 1-10, with 1 being low and 10 being high.

2. Reflect on recent boardroom meetings or interactions. Were there instances where the group members demonstrated emotional self-regulation, managing their own emotions, and responding calmly and thoughtfully to challenging situations? Provide specific examples.

3. Are there any specific challenges or areas where the group could improve their emotional regulation skills? If yes, describe these challenges and discuss potential strategies for improvement.

Section 3: Empathy and Understanding

1. How well does the group collectively demonstrate empathy and understanding towards each other's perspectives, experiences, and emotions during boardroom discussions and decision-making? Rate the group's level of empathy on a scale of 1-10, with 1 being low and 10 being high.

2. Reflect on recent boardroom meetings or interactions. Were there instances where the group members actively listened, considered and valued diverse viewpoints, and responded with empathy? Provide specific examples.

3. Are there any specific challenges or areas where the group could improve their empathy and understanding towards each other? If yes, describe these challenges and discuss potential strategies for improvement.

Section 4: Relationship Management

1. How effectively does the group collectively manage relationships and foster positive interactions within the boardroom? Rate the group's relationship management skills on a scale of 1-10, with 1 being low and 10 being high.

2. Reflect on recent boardroom meetings or interactions. Were there instances where the group members demonstrated strong relationship management skills, such as building rapport, resolving conflicts, or collaborating effectively? Provide specific examples.

3. Are there any specific challenges or areas where the group could improve their relationship management skills? If yes, describe these challenges and discuss potential strategies for improvement.

Section 5: Action Plan

1. Based on the evaluation of the group's emotional intelligence, identify three key areas where the group can collectively improve their emotional intelligence in the boardroom.

2. Discuss potential strategies or initiatives that the group can implement to enhance their emotional intelligence in the identified areas. Assign responsibilities and set timelines if necessary.

3. How will you monitor and measure progress in improving the group's emotional intelligence in the boardroom? Discuss ways to track improvement and consider scheduling periodic

check-ins to reassess the group's emotional intelligence collectively.

Remember to discuss the findings with your board members openly. Then use the insights gained to identify areas for improvement and develop strategies for enhancing the group's collective emotional intelligence. Continuous evaluation and development in this area will contribute to a more harmonious, collaborative, and emotionally intelligent boardroom environment.

Deploying Emotional Intelligence to Navigate Ethical Dilemmas in the Boardroom

In *Moral Choices: An Introduction to Ethics*, Scott B. Rae (2018) wrote, "Ethics are important because they give direction to people and societies who have some sense that they cannot flourish without being moral."

For all humans, ethics constitute moral principles that dictate an individual's conduct. The interplay between emotional intelligence and ethics becomes valuable because it allows individuals to leverage their intelligence ethically, guiding their thoughts and actions while managing emotions to adapt to various environments.

The boardroom is a critical setting where ethical dilemmas can arise due to the intersection of business interests, corporate governance, and stakeholder expectations.

An ethical dilemma is a complex situation that presents a difficult choice between two or more morally conflicting options. They arise when individuals or organizations encounter a conflict between their ethical principles, values, or responsibilities. These dilemmas can arise in both business or personal relationships, but in the professional context, ethical dilemmas often involve decisions that have potential consequences affecting multiple stakeholders, making the decision-making process challenging and thought-provoking.

Ethical dilemmas require individuals to carefully navigate the ethical terrain to determine the best course of action. Often, this involves weighing the potential benefits against the potential harms, considering long-term implications, and balancing competing interests. Successfully resolving an ethical dilemma involves thoughtful consideration, critical analysis, and a commitment to upholding ethical standards, even when faced with difficult choices.

> "Ethics is knowing the difference between
> what you have a right to do and
> what is right to do."
> — Peter Stewart

Here are some common ethical dilemmas that can occur in the boardroom:

Conflicts of interest: Conflict of interest is a common ethical dilemma faced by board directors. Board directors may face conflicts of interest when their personal or financial interests interfere with their duty to act in the best interest of the company and its stakeholders. For example, a board director might have personal relationships or financial stakes that could bias their decision-making process, leading to ethical concerns.

Executive compensation: Executive compensation presents a significant ethical dilemma for boards (Murphy 2013). Board directors must strike a balance between providing fair and competitive compensation for executives while ensuring it aligns with company performance. Excessive or disproportionate compensation can raise ethical concerns, particularly if it fails to consider the interests of other stakeholders or employees.

Whistleblower protection: The board may face ethical dilemmas when handling reports of misconduct or whistleblowing. Balancing the need for transparency and accountability with protecting the identity and well-being of whistleblowers can be challenging. Boards must establish clear processes to handle such reports and ensure that whistleblowers are not subject to retaliation.

Environmental and corporate social responsibility: Ethical dilemmas often arise when deciding on the company's stance and actions regarding social and environmental issues (Jones, Willness & Glavas, 2014). Directors may debate the allocation of resources, such as philanthropic initiatives or sustainability practices, and their impact on long-term profitability. Striking the right balance between financial considerations and broader social responsibilities can be complex.

Risk management: Ethical considerations come into play when making decisions related to risk management. Boards must evaluate risks associated with the company's operations, financial reporting, compliance, and reputation. Ethical dilemmas may arise when weighing the potential impact of risks on stakeholders and deciding on the appropriate level of risk mitigation.

Stakeholder interests: Stakeholder prioritization is a complex ethical dilemma that boards must navigate (Freeman, Harrison & Wicks 2007). Directors need to consider the long-term sustainability of the company, ethical implications of business practices, and the fair distribution of benefits and risks among stakeholders.

Board transparency and accountability: Ethical dilemmas can arise when it comes to board transparency and accountability. Boards must decide how much information to disclose to shareholders and the public, as well as how to ensure transparency in their decision-making processes. Balancing the need for confidentiality and competitive advantage with transparency and accountability can be ethically complex.

Navigating these ethical dilemmas in the boardroom requires a strong ethical framework, transparency, open dialogue, and adherence to legal and regulatory standards. Directors should strive to act with integrity, consider diverse perspectives, and prioritize the long-term sustainability and ethical conduct of the organization.

An ethical framework should be firmly grounded in one or more ethical paradigms to provide a clear and coherent foundation for ethical decision-making. Ethical paradigms serve as the moral compass guiding organizations towards responsible and sustainable decision-making. In the fast-paced and competitive business environment, it is tempting for directors to prioritize profit maximization at any cost. However, ethical paradigms remind us that ethical conduct is not just a legal requirement but a moral obligation. When ethical principles are upheld in the boardroom, it fosters trust among stakeholders, including employees, customers, investors, and the broader community.

Furthermore, ethical decision-making minimizes the risk of legal troubles and reputational damage, which can be catastrophic for any organization. Beyond compliance and risk mitigation, ethical paradigms also contribute to long-term success by fostering a culture of integrity, innovation, and social responsibility. Ultimately, the boardroom should not only be a place for strategic planning but also a forum for ethical deliberation, where the values and principles that underpin a company's operations are given the utmost consideration.

Here are several ethical paradigms that boards can employ to navigate ethical dilemmas:

Truth versus Loyalty

Boards must prioritize truth and transparency as fundamental ethical principles. They are responsible for upholding the integrity and reputation of the organization. In cases where directors or executives are involved in misconduct or ethical violations, the board's primary loyalty should be to the organization and its stakeholders rather than to the individuals involved. Open and honest communication, thorough investigations, and accountability measures should be employed to ensure that the truth prevails and that the organization's interests are safeguarded.

Short-Term versus Long-Term

Boards are entrusted with the long-term sustainability and success of the organization. While there may be pressures to achieve short-term financial goals or immediate profits, boards should prioritize long-term strategic planning that considers the organization's impact on its stakeholders, the environment, and its overall reputation. Ethical decision-making should involve assessing the potential consequences of short-term gains on the organization's long-term health and stability.

Justice versus Mercy

Boards must ensure that justice and fairness are upheld within the organization. This involves implementing policies, procedures, and governance structures that promote equity, diversity, and ethical conduct. However, boards should also be mindful of situations where mercy and compassion may be warranted, such as when addressing ethical lapses by employees or executives. Balancing justice with mercy requires a case-by-case assessment and should be guided by organizational values and principles of fairness.

Individual versus Community

The board's primary ethical responsibility is to the organization and its stakeholders, which often include employees, shareholders, customers, and the broader community. Boards should make decisions that align with the organization's mission and values, taking into account the interests of both individual members and the larger community. Ethical considerations should extend beyond individual board members' interests and focus on the organization's role in promoting the well-being of its broader community.

How Does EI Influence Ethical Decisions?

Ethical decision-making is a critical aspect of leadership and organizational governance. It requires considering the moral implications and consequences of actions, demonstrating integrity, and aligning decisions with ethical principles.

Decision-making in the boardroom can be significantly influenced by the diverse ethical perspectives and varying interpretations of what is morally right among individual directors. Each director brings their unique set of values, principles, and ethical framework to the table, shaping their approach to decision-making. These divergent ethical viewpoints can lead to robust discussions and debates as directors navigate through complex choices, considering the broader implications and potential consequences. Recognizing and appreciating these contrasting ethical perspectives can foster a more comprehensive examination of issues and enable the board to arrive at well-rounded decisions that balance multiple ethical considerations.

Emotional intelligence plays a vital role in influencing ethical decision-making processes by enhancing self-awareness, empathy, and self-regulation. Mahanta and Goswami (2020) explored the role of ethics in emotional intelligence, associating these variables with the organizational commitment relationship. This association underscores the importance of emotional intelligence in fostering loyalty and dedication within the workforce. Based on their conclusions, individuals with higher emotional intelligence tended to have a more profound understanding of ethics within the workplace. They were not only able to recognize morally questionable situations, but could also comprehend the ramifications of unethical conduct.

Here are several ways in which emotional intelligence influences ethical decisions:

Empathetic standpoint: Emotional intelligence encourages empathy, a vital quality for making just choices. Empathetic board members are better equipped to take into account the needs and concerns of everyone, from employees and customers to the local community and beyond. Considering various viewpoints may help directors make fair, inclusive, and economically viable choices.

Awareness and communication: Directors with high EI can recognize and appropriately react to their own and others' emotions, resulting in more honest and considerate interactions. This may help cultivate a culture of openness and responsibility by providing a setting where ethical concerns can be addressed openly.

Tackling stress: Ethical decision-making can be challenging since it often involves balancing opposing priorities, dealing with uncertainty, or taking calculated risks. Emotionally intelligent directors have a greater capacity to deal with stress, allowing them to maintain clarity of mind and make ethical choices under difficult circumstances.

Addressing biases: Additionally, a board member's ability to recognize and control their biases may significantly impact their ability to make moral decisions. Possessing emotional intelligence makes it easier to identify scenarios when strong feelings may influence a decision, or when emotional distance may cause one to ignore the human consequences of a choice.

Fostering resilience: It is essential to have the moral fortitude to stand up for what is right, even if it means risking ridicule or rejection. Emotional intelligence can provide board directors the resilience to keep their moral compass steady and act in the face of pressure.

Emotional intelligence plays a significant role in influencing ethical decisions in the boardroom. Board directors with high emotional intelligence are better at considering multiple perspectives, regulating their emotions, and making ethical choices that benefit stakeholders and align with organizational values. This intentional focus on emotional intelligence creates an environment where ethical considerations are valued, respected, and ingrained in the fabric of the organization. By cultivating a culture that upholds ethical decision-making, organizations can not only enhance their reputation and stakeholder relationships, but also foster a resilient and sustainable business model that withstands the test of time.

Championing Ethical Decision-Making: Strategies for Enterprises and Boardrooms

Based on Ernst and Young's (2020) findings, the crux of moral decision-making lies in a clear and robust organizational purpose. For 18% of leaders, the organization's purpose shapes their ethical compass, around which all tactical and strategic decisions revolve. It is no longer about simply doing things right, but about doing the right things, guided by a well-defined purpose that permeates the entire organization.

The following are the key findings that have emerged from the research:

Modeling behavior: As 14% of leaders assert, it is not just about wielding authority but about demonstrating ethical behaviors, acting as role models, and inspiring others through their actions. It is about creating a leadership narrative where ethical decisions are not outliers, but the norm.

Safe environments: Yet, the idea of a psychologically safe environment is where real innovation emerges. Twelve percent of leaders recognize this as crucial, nurturing spaces where individuals feel empowered to voice their opinions, challenge decisions, and share unique perspectives without fear of backlash. Ethical decisions flourish in these innovative spaces, rooted in the diversity of thought.

Two-way discussions: Communication is not a one-way street; it is an engaging, interactive process, valued by 12% of leaders, where ideas, ethical quandaries, and feedback flow freely from the board to employees and back again, fostering a transparent and inclusive ethical culture.

Promoting ethical practices: For 8% of leaders, this involves innovatively realigning organizational structures and processes—such as hiring, training, and rewards—to support and incentivize ethical decision-making.

Based on these findings, it can be asserted that boards have the potential to pursue ethical decisions by embracing a holistic approach that incorporates ethical considerations into their decision-making processes. This approach should integrate various components, such as:

Develop and communicate ethical standards: Boards should establish clear ethical standards that outline the organization's values, principles, and expectations for ethical conduct. These standards should be communicated to all stakeholders to create a shared understanding of the organization's commitment to ethics.

Strengthen ethical decision-making frameworks: Develop frameworks and processes that explicitly consider ethical implications. This may involve conducting ethical impact assessments, weighing potential consequences, and assessing the alignment of decisions with ethical values and legal requirements. Encourage board directors to engage in ethical discussions and seek diverse perspectives before making decisions.

Establish a strong ethical culture: Foster a culture that values ethical behavior and decision-making at all levels of the organization. This starts with setting clear expectations and standards of conduct, which should be communicated and reinforced through continuing ethics training programs, codes of ethics, and ongoing communication.

Implement ethical oversight and compliance mechanisms: Establish robust oversight and compliance mechanisms to ensure adherence to ethical standards. This includes monitoring and auditing processes, ethical reviews of business practices, enforcing consequences for ethical misconduct, and rewarding ethical practices. Regular assessments help identify areas for improvement and maintain ethical standards.

Enhance board composition and diversity: Boardrooms should strive for diverse and independent board members who bring varied perspectives and experiences. This diversity helps to prevent groupthink and encourages more robust discussions on ethical matters. In particular, board members with expertise in ethics or corporate social responsibility can contribute valuable insights.

Incorporate ethics into strategic planning: Ethics should be integrated into the organization's strategic planning process. Consider the ethical implications of proposed strategies, initiatives, and business practices. Assess the potential risks and benefits to stakeholders and align strategic goals with ethical principles.

Encourage ethical leadership: Boards should lead by example and promote ethical leadership throughout the organization. Board directors should act as ethical role models, demonstrating integrity, transparency, and accountability. Encourage ethical behavior in the executive team and throughout the organization by recognizing and rewarding ethical conduct.

Engage stakeholders and seek input: Involve stakeholders in the decision-making process to understand their perspectives and concerns. This includes shareholders, employees, customers, suppliers, and the wider community. Seek feedback, conduct stakeholder consultations, and consider their input when making ethical decisions.

Transparency and accountability: It is important for board members to maintain transparency in their decision-making process, providing clear justifications for their choices and ensuring accountability for ethical outcomes. This fosters trust and integrity within the boardroom and across the organization.

Regularly review and evaluate ethical performance: Conduct regular reviews and evaluations to assess the board and organization's ethical performance and identify areas for improvement. This can involve internal audits, external assessments, or independent evaluations. Address any identified gaps or shortcomings promptly and with transparency.

Foster a learning culture: Promote continuous learning and improvement in ethical decision-making. Encourage open dialogue, reflection, and ongoing education about ethical issues and emerging trends. Establish mechanisms for learning from ethical dilemmas, mistakes, and successes to enhance future decision-making.

Board induction: As part of the board induction process, it is recommended to include comprehensive training on ethical decision-making. By integrating ethical decision-making training into board induction, organizations can equip new board members with the necessary knowledge and skills to navigate complex ethical dilemmas and make informed, responsible decisions in alignment with the organization's values and stakeholder expectations.

"Ethics and equity and the principles of justice
do not change with the calendar."
− D. H. Lawrence

Boards play a critical role in shaping the ethical direction of an organization. As custodians of governance and strategic decision-making, boards should actively pursue ethical decisions to uphold the highest standards of integrity and accountability. Ethical decisions serve as a compass, guiding boards in navigating complex challenges and dilemmas, ensuring that actions align with the organization's values and the expectations of stakeholders.

Pursuing ethical decisions also helps boards foster a culture of trust, transparency, and fairness, which in turn enhances the organization's reputation, attracts top talent, and strengthens relationships with customers, investors, and the broader community. Through their commitment to ethical decision-making, boards become catalysts for positive change, influencing the organization's behavior and contributing to a sustainable and socially responsible future.

From Emotions to Emotional Intelligence

Even in the boardroom, emotions play a crucial role in shaping perceptions and influencing decisions. This highlights the significance of emotional intelligence in the boardroom setting.

It is important to recognize that despite having a clear understanding of what the right decision should be the emotional state of board members can have a substantial impact on the decision-making process. This dynamic often leads to suboptimal results as emotions can cloud judgment and lead to biased or irrational decision-making. Therefore, developing emotional intelligence skills among board directors becomes imperative to effectively manage and navigate through these emotional influences, ensuring that decisions are made with clarity, objectivity, and a deep understanding of their potential consequences.

After all, decisions swayed by unmanaged emotions can result in adverse consequences for both the decision-maker and others, causing significant damage, some of which may be irreparable.

An exploration into emotion regulation reveals that emotional intelligence can assist individuals in navigating through various contexts and scenarios with different emotional states.

In any given situation or moment, there can be noticeable variations in emotions, which can be categorized as follows:

1. The emotion an individual desires to experience

2. The emotion that is appropriate for the situation

3. The emotion that the individual actually experiences.

The journey from emotions to emotional intelligence signifies a transformative shift in how we perceive and harness our emotional experiences. It is an evolution that moves us from being at the mercy of our emotions to developing a profound understanding and mastery of them. By embracing emotional intelligence, we embark on a path of self-discovery and personal growth that empowers us to navigate the complexities of life with grace, resilience, and wisdom.

The transition begins by recognizing the profound impact that emotions have on our thoughts, behaviors, and relationships. We acknowledge that emotions are not mere fleeting sensations, but powerful messengers that carry valuable insights about our inner world. By cultivating self-awareness, we become attuned to the subtle nuances of our emotions, uncovering their underlying causes and triggers.

Through this heightened self-awareness, we develop the capacity to regulate our emotions effectively. We learn to navigate the ebb and flow of emotional states, choosing our responses with intention and clarity. Instead of reacting impulsively, we cultivate the ability to pause, reflect, and respond in a way that aligns with our values and long-term goals.

Emotional intelligence goes beyond self-mastery. It encompasses the empathetic understanding of others' emotions, enabling us to forge deeper connections and nurture more meaningful relationships. By developing empathy, we recognize the unique experiences and perspectives of those around us, fostering an environment of inclusivity, support, and understanding.

The journey from emotions to emotional intelligence requires deliberate practice and a commitment to growth. It involves cultivating skills such as active listening, effective communication, and conflict resolution, which enable us to navigate interpersonal dynamics with compassion, authenticity, and respect.

As we embrace emotional intelligence, we begin to witness a profound transformation in our personal and professional lives. We become more resilient in the face of challenges, as we draw upon our emotional intelligence to navigate adversity and setbacks. Decision-making becomes more informed and balanced, as we incorporate the wisdom of both the heart and the mind.

From emotions to emotional intelligence, the journey is one of empowerment, growth, and self-discovery. It is a continual process of refining our emotional awareness, regulation, and empathy. By embarking on this journey, we open ourselves to a world of deeper understanding, richer connections, and greater fulfillment in all aspects of life.

Worksheet: EI and Ethical Decision-Making

Use this worksheet as a guide to develop strategies for applying emotional intelligence in ethical decision-making processes. Reflect on each question and provide thoughtful responses. Consider real-life scenarios or hypothetical situations to deepen your understanding.

Section 1: Self-Awareness and Ethical Values

1. Reflect on your personal ethical values and principles. How well do you understand and articulate these values? How do they guide your decision-making in the boardroom?

2. How can self-awareness contribute to ethical decision-making in the boardroom? Consider the importance of recognizing your own biases, values, and emotions in relation to ethical dilemmas.

3. Think of a recent boardroom decision where self-awareness played a significant role in your ethical decision-making process. How did your self-awareness influence the outcome?

Section 2: Managing Emotions in Ethical Decision-Making

1. Reflect on a past boardroom decision where you effectively managed your emotions to make an ethical choice. How did emotional intelligence play a role in maintaining clarity and objectivity?

Section 3: Action Plan

1. Based on the insights gained from this worksheet, identify two key areas where you can enhance your use of emotional intelligence to improve ethical decision-making in the boardroom.

2. Outline an action plan with specific steps and timelines to develop and strengthen your emotional intelligence in the identified areas. Consider incorporating training, self-reflection exercises, or seeking feedback from colleagues.

3. How will you assess and measure your progress in using emotional intelligence to improve ethical decision-making? Discuss methods for tracking improvements and consider seeking feedback from your colleagues.

Improving Boardroom Dynamics With Emotional Intelligence

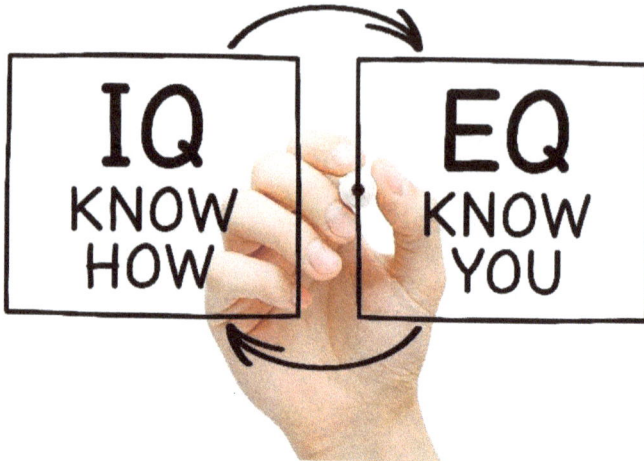

Boardroom dynamics refer to the complex interactions, relationships, and power dynamics among board members within an organization. Understanding and managing these dynamics is crucial for effective governance and decision-making.

The boardroom is a unique environment where individuals with diverse backgrounds, expertise, and perspectives come together to oversee the strategic direction of the organization. In essence, boards are a microcosm of humanity itself.

As the psychoanalyst Wilfred Bion noted, all groups form for a specific purpose. For boards, the objective spans advising management, acting as a beacon during crises, safeguarding assets, managing CEO succession, and much more. The effectiveness of a group hinges partly on its dynamics—the harmonious or discordant interplay of personalities as they go about their duties. Boards that excel share a common trait: the ability to align, if not agree, on their core purpose.

Boards tangled in counterproductive dynamics often find themselves mired in interpersonal or political quagmires, while others might succumb to the monoculture of groupthink. Improving board dynamics requires cultivating an awareness of undercurrents in board meetings. One can enhance their understanding of a situation by looking for cues in non-verbal communication, informal roles, the broader context, and unspoken issues.

As emphasized by Deloitte's Sharon Allen (2020), "Boards can decide to invest in strengthening their own dynamics just as they might decide to invest in any other asset that would strengthen the balance sheet."

To effectively manage boardroom dynamics, it is essential to establish effective communication channels, promote active listening, and encourage constructive debate and collaboration among board members. Regular board evaluations and self-assessments can also help identify areas of improvement and ensure that the board is functioning effectively (Solomon & Solomon 2020).

Exploring the Causes Impacting Boardroom Dynamics

Citing research conducted by Griffin et al. (2017), it is pretty clear that boardroom dynamics present a significant challenge, as indicated by director dissatisfaction. Only 64% of directors strongly believe their board is receptive to new perspectives, while just half strongly believe that the skills of all board members are effectively utilized. Furthermore, less than half (46%) strongly believe that their board tolerates dissenting opinions.

Boardroom dynamics can be influenced by various causes that impact the interactions, decision-making processes, and overall effectiveness of the board. Often the dynamics are influenced by external or wider factors encompassing organizational events, the business climate, and the socio-political landscape. Even board routines like the sequence of agenda items can shape this context, as one decision may impact subsequent ones.

As well as these external factors, often internal aspects—such as individual personalities and behaviors—can have a major impact on boardroom dynamics. Conflicting personalities, conflicts of interest, and the distribution of power and influence can significantly impact decision-making processes (Huse 2005). Considering that boardrooms likely comprise people with strong personalities and even stronger convictions, this represents a challenging dynamic to overcome. Effective boards have mechanisms in place to manage power dynamics, such as clear roles and responsibilities, open communication channels, and the ability to challenge and question decisions.

Research suggests that the composition of the board, including the diversity of its members, can significantly impact the decision-making process and overall boardroom dynamics. For example, studies have shown that gender diversity on boards can enhance collaboration, creativity, and decision-making effectiveness (Erhardt et al., 2003). Furthermore, the behavior and leadership style of the board chair or CEO can greatly influence the dynamics and functioning of the board.

Additionally, boardroom dynamics are influenced by the culture and norms within the organization, which can shape the behavior, attitudes, and decision-making processes of board members. Boards that foster a culture of trust, open communication, and accountability are more likely to have constructive and productive dynamics (Tricker 2015).

Historical disputes and unresolved issues from the past can cast a shadow over the boardroom, resulting in lingering tensions. These historical disputes might stem from disagreements that were never fully addressed, decisions made without complete consensus, or contentious transactions. They can create an undercurrent of tension and exacerbate conflicts within the board. Recognizing and dealing with these issues, or the proverbial "elephant in the room," is essential for a healthy board dynamic.

Fundamental disagreements over the strategic direction or specific actions proposed by the board can also spark tension and conflict and influence boardroom dynamics. These disagreements can take many forms, from differing viewpoints on the best course of action to conflicting visions for the company's future, or clashes between directors' personal interests and the organization's objectives. These conflicts often emerge during critical decision-making processes, where the stakes are high and diverse perspectives collide.

Additionally, external pressures and stakeholder expectations play a role in boardroom dynamics. These may include regulatory requirements, shareholder activism, or public scrutiny. Stakeholder expectations for ethical conduct, accountability, and transparency also shape boardroom behavior. Though not always inherently negative, external pressures can create both challenges and opportunities, affecting decision-making and dynamics within the boardroom.

"There is nothing immoral about having an emotional problem to solve. No need to feel ashamed; it is not a weakness. Indeed, it is a weakness to be unable to admit to yourself that you are in distress."
— Wayne Payne

Trust in relationships is a key factor that determines the quality of boardroom dynamics. Building and maintaining trust among board directors and between the board and management promotes open dialogue, constructive dissent, and effective decision-making. Lack of trust can lead to conflicts, skepticism, and a breakdown in collaboration.

Improving boardroom dynamics demands intentionally cultivating what French and Simpson (2018) term "evenly suspended attention": a comprehensive awareness of the undertones in a board meeting. This awareness helps to decipher the boardroom's emotional state, offering insights into key dynamics.

Board members often adopt informal roles such as the cheerleader or devil's advocate, which can significantly influence group dynamics. Identifying these roles and understanding their impact on performance can aid in creating more effective board dynamics.

Enhancing Boardroom Dynamics

Boardroom dynamics play a critical role in the effectiveness of corporate governance and decision-making processes. When boardroom dynamics are positive and collaborative, it can lead to improved board performance, better decision outcomes, and ultimately, organizational success. On the other hand, negative or dysfunctional dynamics can hinder effective governance and lead to suboptimal decision-making. Therefore, it is essential to identify strategies to improve boardroom dynamics and foster a positive and productive environment.

Communication and Transparency

Research shows that open and transparent communication in the boardroom can enhance board effectiveness and decision-making (Huse 2007). Effective communication ensures that information flows freely, ideas are shared, and different perspectives are heard and considered. Encouraging active participation and creating opportunities for board members to express their opinions and concerns can promote a culture of trust and collaboration.

Board Composition

Another strategy to improve boardroom dynamics is to focus on board composition and diversity. Research indicates that diverse boards are more likely to exhibit higher levels of innovation, creativity, and effective governance (Carter et al. 2003). By promoting diversity in terms of age, gender, ethnicity, industry background, and skills, boards can benefit from a wider range of insights and perspectives, thereby enhancing the quality of discussions and decision-making processes.

Trust and Respect

Fostering a culture of respect and trust within the boardroom is crucial, as when board members feel valued and respected, they are more likely to actively engage in discussions and contribute their ideas and expertise. Building trust among board members can be achieved through transparent decision-making processes, maintaining confidentiality when necessary, and promoting a supportive and collaborative atmosphere (Solomon & Solomon 2020).

Board Evaluation and Professional Development

Regular board evaluations and self-assessments provide an opportunity to assess the performance and effectiveness of individual board members, as well as the overall functioning of the board. By identifying strengths, weaknesses, and areas for improvement, boards can take targeted actions to enhance their dynamics and performance.

In addition, providing professional development opportunities can enhance the knowledge, skills, and competencies of board members, enabling them to make informed decisions and contribute effectively to board discussions. Investing in board education and training demonstrates a commitment to board effectiveness and can strengthen relationships and collaboration among board members (Solomon & Solomon 2020).

Innovation at Risk From a Lack of Debate

Board meetings with no robust debate may be just as detrimental to a company as those with frequent disagreement. When all directors agree on everything, the result is a monolithic approach, and may indicate a lack of diversity in the board. This may lead to complacency, lack of individuality, and a restrictive culture that stifles creativity. To solve this issue, boards should assess its makeup and think about ways to increase diversity, such as by appointing directors from a wide range of backgrounds and fields of expertise.

Finding an Appropriate Middle Ground

Finding a balance in boardroom dynamics entails avoiding personal conflicts and heated debates. Directors may be reluctant to bring up sensitive issues when disputes become personal attacks, hindering decision-making and inhibiting open dialogue. The challenge is creating a boardroom culture that is just the appropriate amount of combative without being unduly accommodating. Good boards know how to diffuse tension before it becomes a destructive confrontation, as Andrew Kakabadse of Henley Business School emphasizes, cited by Rathod (2018).

Understanding the Board Chair's Vital Function

Undoubtedly, the chair's role is pivotal in improving boardroom dynamics and fostering a positive and productive environment. The chair's leadership and facilitation skills significantly influence the tone and effectiveness of board discussions and decision-making processes.

First, the chairperson plays a key role in setting the right boardroom culture and creating an atmosphere of trust, respect, and open communication. When faced with dominant personalities in the boardroom, it is crucial for the chair to foster an environment of open and productive debate where all directors have equal opportunities to contribute. They should encourage active participation from all board members by creating a safe space where differing viewpoints are respected and valued. This can be done by setting ground rules for the meeting, such as allocating equal speaking time to each director and ensuring that interruptions are minimized. By promoting fairness and equal opportunity for participation, the chair helps prevent dominating personalities from stifling the contributions of others or monopolizing the discussion.

Second, the chair facilitates productive discussions by managing the agenda, encouraging active participation, and ensuring that discussions remain focused and constructive. They can ask open-ended questions, encourage thoughtful debates, challenge assumptions, prioritize evidence-based arguments, and mediate conflicts when they arise, aiming to maintain a balanced and inclusive atmosphere.

Third, the chairperson can promote transparency by providing timely and accurate information to board members and ensuring that they have access to the necessary resources for decision-making. They can also foster accountability by setting clear expectations and holding board members accountable for their responsibilities.

The chair must have certain qualities to do their job effectively, such as excellent communication skills, the ability to serve as a link between management and the board, the know-how to deal with a wide range of characters, a consultative style when necessary, as well as the ability to distill essential information from convoluted debates.

Preserving Harmony in the Group

The role of the chair is a critical leadership position within the boardroom and solid succession planning is essential for maintaining continuity, strategic alignment, and strong governance. Well-executed chair succession planning contributes to better board performance and organizational outcomes.

One of the key benefits of chair succession planning is the smooth transition of leadership. By identifying and grooming potential successors in advance, organizations can avoid sudden leadership vacuums and ensure a seamless transfer of responsibilities. This allows for the preservation of institutional knowledge and expertise while providing the incoming chair with a comprehensive understanding of the organization's strategic goals and challenges.

Furthermore, chair succession planning facilitates the development of leadership capabilities within the board. It provides an opportunity to identify and nurture talented individuals who have the potential to assume the role in the future. This proactive approach to succession planning helps cultivate a pool of capable leaders who are well-prepared to guide the organization effectively.

Implementing a structured succession planning process also demonstrates the organization's commitment to strong governance practices and ensures a fair and transparent selection process. By establishing clear criteria and performance expectations for the chair role, the organization can attract and retain highly qualified candidates who possess the necessary skills, experience, and values.

Maintaining Open Lines of Communication and Participation

All board members should be able to communicate effectively both within and outside of board meetings. Directors are more likely to remain active and contribute to the company's success if they have frequent opportunities to expand their knowledge of the industry and its inner workings. This gives them the ability to raise valid objections based on firsthand information. Organizations may help directors keep in touch and up to date in real-time by providing them with individualized messaging systems and round-the-clock access to the board and committee material without compromising data security.

Worksheet: Improving Boardroom Dynamics with EI

Reflect on each question and provide thoughtful responses. Consider real-life scenarios or hypothetical situations to deepen your understanding.

1. Reflect on your self-awareness in the boardroom. How well do you understand and manage your own emotions? How does your self-awareness impact your interactions and contributions to the boardroom dynamics?

2. Reflect on your communication skills in the boardroom. How effectively do you convey your thoughts, actively listen, and respond to others? How does your communication style impact boardroom dynamics?

3. How can emotional intelligence support conflict resolution and collaboration in the boardroom? Consider the role of empathy, perspective-taking, and open dialogue in resolving conflicts and building trust.

4. Based on the insights gained from this worksheet, identify two key areas where you can enhance your use of emotional intelligence to improve boardroom dynamics.

5. Outline an action plan with specific steps and timelines to develop and strengthen your emotional intelligence in the identified areas.

Promoting a Board Culture of Emotional Intelligence

The propensity to make money at all costs is often blamed for many global problems, such as climate change, environmental damage, human rights violations, and exploitation of workers. In the present era, there is a growing questioning of the paradigm that companies should solely prioritize the increase of shareholder wealth. To truly instill change, directors should lead by example.

> "Your time is limited, so don't waste it living someone else's life. Don't be trapped by dogma—which is living with the results of other people's thinking. Don't let the noise of others' opinions drown out your own inner voice. And most important, have the courage to follow your heart and intuition."
> — Steve Jobs

Boards are usually comprised of a limited group of members, typically ranging from eight to twelve individuals on average. To promote a board culture of emotional intelligence, it is essential to start at the top. Board directors should lead by example, demonstrating and embracing emotional intelligence in their own actions and interactions. This includes actively listening to diverse perspectives, considering the emotional impact of decisions, and practicing open and transparent communication.

Incorporating emotional intelligence assessments into board evaluations can also provide valuable insights into the emotional dynamics within the boardroom. This can help identify areas for improvement and guide the development of targeted strategies to enhance emotional intelligence at the board level.

Board directors and decision-makers cannot do their jobs without trust; it is the currency that helps them succeed, build connections, and overcome obstacles. However, trust is not always there and has to be fostered. This is where emotional intelligence comes in.

In line with the acumen of Women Serve on Boards (2022), "Emotionally intelligent directors are better at motivating the people around them. They can provide effective communication, leadership and inspiration for others." As society explores innovative approaches to conducting business, the current juncture presents an opportune moment to contemplate the ideal leaders for large companies and the requisite skill sets they need to thrive in the future. A culture infused with emotional intelligence might be the answer to a better world.

"I am not afraid of an army of lions led by a sheep; I am afraid of an army of sheep led by a lion."
— Alexander the Great

Decoding Board Culture: Understanding its Essence and Significance

Board culture refers to the shared values, norms, and behaviors that shape the interactions and dynamics within a board of directors. It encompasses the collective attitudes, communication patterns, decision-making processes, and overall climate that influence the board's effectiveness and governance outcomes. Establishing a healthy and productive board culture is critical for promoting collaboration, trust, and ethical conduct among directors.

Board culture significantly impacts board performance and organizational success. A positive board culture characterized by openness, mutual respect, and constructive dissent fosters better decision-making, strategic alignment, and risk management. Conversely, a dysfunctional board culture marked by conflicts, lack of transparency, or dominant personalities can hinder effective governance and impede organizational progress.

To cultivate a positive board culture, several key elements can be considered. First and foremost, it is essential to establish a shared sense of purpose and mission that aligns with the organization's values and objectives. This helps directors stay focused, engaged, and committed to the organization's goals.

Open and transparent communication is another critical aspect of fostering positive board culture, a point highlighted in research by Kiel and Nicholson (2003). Encouraging open dialogue, active listening, and respectful debate allows for diverse perspectives to be heard and considered.

Furthermore, promoting a culture of trust and accountability is vital. When directors trust each other and feel safe to express their opinions, it fosters a collaborative environment where ideas can be freely exchanged. Accountability ensures that directors are responsible for their actions and decisions, reinforcing ethical conduct and organizational integrity.

In all instances, a board's culture serves as an invisible playbook, subtly directing the boardroom's dialogue, decision-making, and interpersonal dynamics. This invisible playbook combines attitudes, unspoken expectations, shared norms, values, and elements like the board's agenda, shaping the contours of director discussions and the level of engagement and trust. The leadership style of the board chair or CEO can significantly sway the board's culture.

Cultural dynamics can differ significantly from one geographic region to another. For instance, in certain regions, a straightforward and candid approach might be the norm, while in others, the boardroom might favor a more tactful, "diplomatic" approach. Barring any seismic changes to the board composition—such as mergers or the inclusion of directors backed by activists—the evolution of board culture tends to be gradual, given the sporadic nature of board interactions.

Recognizing and understanding its culture empowers a board to assess how this impacts its performance and contemplate the necessity of potential cultural shifts. Establishing a shared language around the culture and pinpointing the directors' preferred styles facilitates mutual comprehension among board members, enabling them to adapt to each other's preferences and make more informed decisions when evaluating the cultural compatibility of prospective director candidates.

Tackling the Biases Impeding a Valuable Boardroom Culture

Biases refer to systematic and unconscious patterns of thinking and decision-making that have an impact on individuals' perceptions, judgments, and behaviors. These biases have the potential to shape individual preferences, beliefs, and actions, often without individuals being consciously aware of their influence. While biases can function as cognitive shortcuts that aid in processing information more efficiently, they can also act as obstacles, hindering one's capacity to embrace change and impeding endeavors to transform boardroom culture.

In the context of changing boardroom culture, biases can manifest in various ways:

Authority bias: It is fairly common for boards to rely heavily on certain directors due to their expertise, which can lead to an "authority bias." Boards can become overly reliant on specific opinions, undermining others' input and their own responsibility to contribute. To counter authority bias, boards should ensure that every director contributes to each discussion. Additional educational opportunities can empower board members to share their views and question prevalent opinions.

Invitation-only bias: Very often, the prevailing bias towards an invitation-only culture in the boardroom is fueled by the lack of transparency and diversity surrounding the selection process for board member positions. The system of selecting board members heavily favors individuals with personal connections and established networks. This practice is still widely embraced among ASX 100 and government boards.

Groupthink: Affecting most group dynamics across all social settings, groupthink arises when boards prioritize harmony over constructive disagreement, suppressing dissenting views. This leads to decision-making that does not fully consider all perspectives. The board's assessment process can help mitigate groupthink by ensuring directors feel free to express their views. Additionally, introducing outside advisors can bring fresh perspectives into the boardroom.

Status quo bias: Boards often prefer established norms and resist change, creating a "status quo bias," which can prevent them from embracing innovation or making necessary strategic shifts. To overcome status quo bias, boards can bring in outside experts, revamp strategic meeting agendas, or organize visits to innovation hubs.

Confirmation bias: Like all individuals, directors can display "confirmation bias," which values information supporting their pre-existing beliefs and downplays contradicting evidence. Diversity is the best remedy for confirmation bias, since boards that prioritize compatible viewpoints unknowingly reinforce their biases. Instead, promoting rigorous debates among directors with different views can lead to more comprehensive decision-making.

Anchoring bias: This bias occurs when directors rely too heavily on the first piece of information they receive (the "anchor") when making decisions, even if that information is unrelated or irrelevant. In the boardroom, this can lead to a fixation on initial data or proposals, causing directors to overlook important and potentially better alternatives. Recognizing and mitigating anchoring bias is essential for effective boardroom dynamics, as it encourages more open-minded and flexible discussions, enabling boards to make well-informed decisions that drive organizational success.

Availability bias: Making informed decisions is a critical function of a board. However, sometimes directors can overestimate the importance of information that is readily available to them, often due to its recentness or its vividness in memory. This type of bias can lead to a skewed perspective on risks and opportunities, as directors may give disproportionate weight to the most recent or memorable events, overlooking broader trends or long-term considerations. Directors should make strategic choices based on a comprehensive assessment of available data and insights.

Self-serving bias: Some board members might have a psychological tendency to attribute positive outcomes or successes to their own abilities, decisions, or contributions while attributing negative outcomes or failures to external factors or circumstances beyond their control. This bias can manifest in various ways, such as when directors take credit for a company's success without acknowledging the role of other stakeholders or when they deflect responsibility for strategic missteps onto external economic conditions or market fluctuations. Self-serving bias can have significant implications for decision-making and accountability within the boardroom, potentially leading to a lack of transparency and accountability, which can ultimately impact the organization's overall performance and long-term sustainability. Recognizing and mitigating self-serving bias is crucial for fostering a more responsible and effective board.

Infusing Boardroom Culture with Emotional Intelligence

A boardroom culture that is weaved with emotional intelligence can create a setting that values and encourages diverse viewpoints, promotes honesty and productive debate, and ultimately results in more sound judgments.

Recognizing and accommodating varied behavioral preferences: Having board members who can put themselves in the shoes of others and empathize with their thoughts and feelings makes for a more cooperative and productive meeting. This method encourages candid discussion and comprehension, facilitating a speedy and amicable resolution of any issues that may arise.

Focusing on relationship building and self-awareness: To move beyond the propensity to favor and elect individuals from their inner circles, board members should engage with diverse professional communities, organizations, and networks to expand their connections and increase exposure to potential candidates from diverse backgrounds. EI can help facilitate genuine connections and build relationships based on empathy and mutual understanding. When selecting a new board member, it is vital to focus on introspection and reflection on personal connections and networks that may contribute to the bias. By recognizing these biases, directors can make a conscious effort to overcome them.

Encouraging discussions and constructive dissent: Building a culture that welcomes open dissent is crucial in the boardroom. Here, respect and trust act as the adhesive that maintains unity, despite disagreements. A constructive dissenting voice can lead to improved decision-making and protect against groupthink, a common pitfall in corporate governance. Research indicates that high-performing companies often have contentious boards that view dissent as obligatory, with no subject considered too taboo for discussion.

Incorporating EI into board policies: Incorporating EI concepts into board policy is equally important. This could include provisions in the code of conduct emphasizing the importance of listening to and being empathetic towards others. Conflict resolution standards that highlight emotional understanding might also be included.

Adapting to emotional dynamics: Reading and responding to emotional cues inside the boardroom is critical to integrating EI. By perceiving and responding to emotional cues from individuals, directors have the potential to enhance their decision-making, improve their communication skills, and contribute to fostering a more positive atmosphere within the boardroom.

Leveraging EI in board evaluations and recruitment: Make emotional intelligence a key factor in judging board members' performance and selection requirements in order to guarantee they can contribute positively to the boardroom culture.

Providing EI training: Not everyone is naturally skilled in emotional intelligence, but it can be developed through training and practice. Consider offering workshops or seminars on topics such as self-awareness, empathy, and conflict resolution. These can help board directors to better understand themselves and others, and to communicate more effectively.

Recognize and reward EI: Finally, it is important to recognize and reward emotional intelligence within the organization. This can be done through formal recognition programs or simply by acknowledging when someone has demonstrated EI in a particular situation. By doing so, the company sends a clear message that emotional intelligence is valued within the organization.

Strengthening the Board Culture with Trust

Trust is the fuel that powers productive boardroom activities, including making decisions, working together, and achieving organizational goals. Ninety-four percent of the worldwide board members and executives polled by Deloitte (2023) ranked trust as "important" to their organization's success, while the remaining 6% ranked it as "somewhat important." However, only 39% claimed their company had reached high trust maturity and often discussed trust issues at board and management meetings.

> "The glue that holds all relationships together—
>
> including the relationship between the leader and the
>
> led—is trust, and trust is based on integrity."
>
> — Brian Tracy

Trust is built when leaders display sincerity, integrity, openness, and honesty in all they do and speak. They make it such that everyone on the board feels comfortable being honest about their thoughts and feelings with one another. Emotional intelligence promotes trust and cooperation by creating an environment where everyone feels their ideas and opinions are valued.

This is especially important in critical circumstances, as emphasized by Irene Chang Britt, a seasoned director who participates in four different boards: "It's proven critical to have built trust between board and management far in advance of facing the crisis. Not just trust in competence and skill, but trust in mission and intent" (Shalett 2020).

As such, trust is not a one-time achievement, but an ongoing process.

Emotional intelligence helps leaders navigate the trust feedback loop, which involves continuously assessing and monitoring trust levels, actively seeking feedback, and promptly addressing any emerging trust issues.

By integrating emotional intelligence into boardroom practices, directors can build the foundation of a culture of continuous improvement and trust-building, reinforcing positive trust dynamics over time.

Worksheet: Promoting a Board Culture of EI

Reflect on each question and provide thoughtful responses. Consider real-life scenarios or hypothetical situations to deepen your understanding.

Section 1: Assessing Current Board Culture

1. Reflect on the current board culture. How would you describe the overall board culture? What are the strengths and areas for improvement?

2. How can board members and senior leaders promote a culture of emotional intelligence? Discuss the responsibility and influence of leaders in setting the tone for emotional intelligence within the boardroom.

3. Reflect on a board leader or senior member who exemplifies emotional intelligence. How do their actions and behaviors positively impact the board's overall dynamics and effectiveness?

4. Identify three actions or behaviors that you can personally adopt to lead by example and promote emotional intelligence within the board. Explain how each action or behavior can contribute to the board's emotional intelligence.

Leading Change with EI through Strategic Leadership

In *Something Needs to Change Around Here*, Liz Weber (2010) highlights that, "Leaders move among the various stages each day. But effective leaders move among the right stages at the right times." In other words, one of the greatest avenues leaders should pursue is a clear and innovative strategy, which often translates into strategic leadership.

Reynolds (2022) from Harvard University defines strategic leadership as, "when managers use their creative problem-solving skills and strategic vision to help team members and an organization achieve long-term goals."

Complementary to a strategic leadership style, emotional intelligence is far-reaching, bestowing leaders with enhanced self-awareness, fostering a culture of accountability, nurturing effective communication, and building foundations of trust. Emotional intelligence equips leaders to confront challenges head-on and yield positive outcomes by representing the avenue that enables them to process their emotions constructively.

Distinguishing the Role and Effectiveness of Strategic Leadership in Comparison to Other Leadership Styles

Strategic leadership plays a pivotal role in shaping an organization's direction and achieving its long-term objectives. It stands apart from other leadership styles due to its emphasis on vision, adaptability, and proactive decision-making. By distinguishing the unique characteristics and highlighting the effectiveness of this leadership style in comparison to others, one can gain a deeper understanding of its significance in today's dynamic business landscape.

At its core, strategic leadership is about envisioning the future and charting a course towards success. Strategic leaders possess a forward-thinking mindset, continuously scanning the external environment for emerging opportunities and potential threats. They develop a clear vision and set ambitious goals that inspire and align the organization.

Unlike other leadership styles that focus primarily on day-to-day operations, strategic leadership takes a holistic and long-term view. It involves analyzing market trends, identifying industry disruptions, and making informed choices to position the organization for sustainable growth. Strategic leaders are adept at managing complexity, making tough decisions, and allocating resources strategically.

> "We need leaders who can meet and adapt to
> new challenges, build strategic partnerships,
> build and sustain human capital organizations,
> and have the courage to act and
> react to the challenges."
> – Thomas Narofsky

One of the key differentiators of strategic leadership is its adaptability. Strategic leaders are agile and responsive to change, adjusting their strategies and tactics as circumstances evolve. They encourage innovation, foster a culture of continuous learning, and empower their teams to embrace change. By remaining flexible and open to new possibilities, strategic leaders are able to steer their organizations through uncertainties and capitalize on emerging opportunities.

The effectiveness of strategic leadership lies in its ability to create a shared sense of purpose and engage stakeholders at all levels. Strategic leaders communicate the organization's vision and values effectively, inspiring others to contribute their best efforts. They promote collaboration, build strong relationships, and leverage diverse perspectives to drive innovation and achieve collective goals.

Comparing strategic leadership to other leadership styles provides valuable insights into the unique characteristics and approaches of strategic leaders:

Democratic leadership: In contrast to strategic leadership, democratic leaders emphasize inclusivity and collaboration in decision-making. They solicit input from team members and consider their opinions before making a final decision. While strategic leaders also value input and buy-in, they focus on communicating and influencing others to embrace the organization's strategic vision.

Autocratic leadership: Autocratic leaders exhibit a top-down approach, where decisions are made solely by the leader without seeking input from their team members. Strategic leaders, on the other hand, maintain a clear strategic vision for the company but still value team member input, provided it aligns with the vision and encourages innovation and progress.

Servant leadership: Servant leaders delegate authority to their team members, often allowing them to take the lead in decision-making and giving them significant autonomy. In contrast, while strategic leaders trust their team and value objective thinking, they balance this with upholding the strategic vision and prioritizing company growth in order to drive organizational success.

While different leadership styles have their merits, strategic leadership stands out for its focus on long-term success, adaptability, and alignment of actions with a compelling vision. In today's complex and rapidly changing business environment, organizations need strategic leaders who can navigate uncertainties, capitalize on opportunities, and create a sustainable competitive advantage.

Strategic Leadership in the Boardroom

Strategic leadership in the boardroom refers to the ability of board directors to provide guidance, direction, and oversight in driving the organization's long-term vision and strategic goals. It involves setting a clear strategic direction, making informed decisions, and effectively allocating resources to achieve desired outcomes.

According to Hitt, Ireland, and Hoskisson (2019), strategic leaders at the board level play a pivotal role in shaping the organization's strategy, monitoring its execution, and ensuring alignment with stakeholders' expectations. They provide valuable insights, challenge assumptions, and guide the organization through complex and uncertain environments.

Effective strategic leadership requires a deep understanding of the organization's internal and external landscape, industry trends, competitive dynamics, and emerging opportunities. It involves a forward-thinking mindset, the ability to anticipate and adapt to changes, and the capacity to make informed and timely decisions.

Furthermore, strategic leaders in the boardroom foster a culture of innovation, collaboration, and risk management. They encourage open dialogue, diverse perspectives, and critical thinking to drive strategic thinking and ensure robust decision-making processes.

Combining Strategic Thinking and Emotional Intelligence: The Ultimate Leadership Recipe

Extensive research has unequivocally demonstrated emotional intelligence's role as a robust performance indicator. Approximately 90% of high achievers exhibit remarkable levels of emotional intelligence, solidifying their position as a paramount factor.

This revelation has not gone unnoticed by astute recruiters, who are increasingly attuned to the profound impact of emotional intelligence. In fact, a study conducted by CareerBuilder (2011) revealed that an impressive 71% of surveyed professionals hold emotional intelligence in higher regard than intellectual intelligence

(IQ). They recognize that individuals possessing elevated emotional intelligence remain composed and resilient when faced with pressure, adeptly navigate conflicts to resolution, and exhibit a genuine capacity for empathy towards their colleagues.

Overall, the synergy of strategic thinking and emotional intelligence can greatly amplify the effectiveness and influence of leaders. When these two skills are combined, they create a powerful foundation for navigating complex challenges and facilitating meaningful growth for individuals and organizations.

Research by Boyatzis and McKee (2005) highlights the importance of emotional intelligence in strategic thinking. They argue that emotional intelligence enhances cognitive abilities, allowing individuals to think more creatively, consider multiple perspectives, and make well-rounded decisions. EI enables board directors to effectively manage relationships, build trust, and influence stakeholders, which are critical aspects of strategic leadership.

The benefits of this integration will be explored through the following subsections:

Enhancing Decision-Making

Strategic thinking empowers directors to analyze data, assess risks and opportunities, and develop well-informed strategies. By incorporating emotional intelligence, they can factor in the human element, understanding the emotions and motivations of individuals involved in the decision-making process. Such empathetic insights allow them to make decisions considering the logical aspects and the potential impact on stakeholders' well-being and engagement. This holistic approach enables boards to make more balanced and sustainable decisions that consider not only financial outcomes, but also the organization's reputation, ethical implications, and long-term goals.

Fostering Creativity and Innovation

Through the advent of emotional intelligence, directors can tap into their stakeholders' and team members' diverse perspectives, fostering an environment that encourages innovative thinking, collaboration, and open communication. Eventually, this synergy generates unique solutions that go beyond traditional approaches.

Cultivating Effective Relationships

By understanding and managing one's own emotions, as well as being attuned to the emotions of others, directors can establish rapport, trust, and credibility with all stakeholders. The result is a safe and supportive space for open dialogue, active listening, and constructive feedback. Subsequently, a strategic approach provides a framework for aligning these relationships with the broader objectives, ensuring that they contribute to the organization's overall success.

Adapting to Change and Complexity

Strategic thinking equips directors with the ability to assess and respond to changes in the external environment, identify emerging trends, and adjust strategies accordingly. Emotional intelligence complements this by enabling them to navigate the complexities of human dynamics during times of change. It helps directors guide their teams through transitions, manage resistance, and foster resilience in uncertainty.

Maximizing Personal Growth

Integrating strategic thinking and emotional intelligence allows for continuous personal and professional development. Directors can cultivate self-awareness and a growth mindset by leveraging strengths and mitigating weaknesses. This self-reflection, coupled with strategic thinking, empowers directors to identify areas for improvement, embrace new learning opportunities, and refine their approaches over time.

Uncovering Examples of Strategic Leadership

Many leaders exemplify some of the qualities found in great strategic leadership, serving as inspiring examples for others to follow:

Oprah Winfrey began her career as a Nashville television station's first Black local news anchor. Eventually, she became one of the world's wealthiest businesswomen as the CEO of Harpo Inc., a multimedia production company. While Forbes has hailed her as the most powerful businesswoman globally for her business acumen, Oprah is best known for her humble role as a daytime talk show host. Over 25 seasons on the set of *Oprah*, she displayed a down-to-earth, relatable communication style that embodied attentive listening, empathy, compassion, and the remarkable ability to connect with people from radically different backgrounds.

Jacinda Ardern, the former Prime Minister of New Zealand, has garnered international applause for her substantial leadership skills and steady hand during times of crisis. Ardern's adept handling of the of the Covid-19 pandemic, which resulted in relatively low infection levels in the country, has been particularly noteworthy. Industry professionals commend her for her focus on "we" instead of "I," and her ability to actively listen to expert advice and translate it into action. Moreover, Ardern's willingness to acknowledge her strengths and weaknesses engenders trust and strengthens her leadership.

Jeff Bezos, the Chairman and former CEO of Amazon, is recognized for being open to big ideas. Under Bezos's visionary leadership, Amazon transformed from an online bookstore into the world's largest internet company by revenue, while also becoming a leading provider of virtual assistants and cloud infrastructure services. From expanding Amazon's offerings to streaming movies to venturing into sub-orbital spaceflight through his company Blue Origin, Bezos's empire continues to grow due to his unwavering commitment to exploring new frontiers.

Worksheet: Leading Change with EI Through Strategic Leadership

Reflect on each question and provide thoughtful responses. Consider real-life scenarios or hypothetical situations to deepen your understanding.

Section 1: Assessing the Need for Change

1. Identify a change initiative or situation where strategic leadership and emotional intelligence are crucial. Consider the current state, the desired future state, and the reasons driving the need for change.

2. Reflect on a past experience where emotional intelligence played a significant role in leading change effectively. How did your emotional intelligence skills contribute to navigating challenges and facilitating positive outcomes?

3. How does emotional intelligence contribute to setting a clear vision and strategy for change?

4. Recall a situation in which your emotional intelligence skills were instrumental in effectively managing resistance or conflict during a period of change. Reflect on how your ability to regulate your emotions and demonstrate empathy towards different viewpoints played a vital role in reaching a positive resolution.

Uncovering the Challenges in Applying Emotional Intelligence in the Boardroom

"Obstacles are those frightful things you see
when you take your eyes off your goal."
— Henry Ford.

Inside all boardrooms, where strategic decisions shape the fate of organizations, complex dynamics often elude the traditional lens of analysis and expertise. This is a space where emotions intertwine with rationality; where the intangible forces of human interaction undeniably influence the trajectory of success or failure.

Twenty years ago, Jeffrey A. Sonnenfeld thoroughly addressed the prevailing question "What makes great boards great?" in a Harvard Business Review article of the same name:

> So if following good-governance regulatory recipes doesn't produce good boards, what does? The key isn't structural, it's social. [...] What distinguishes exemplary boards is that they are robust, effective social systems. The highest-performing companies have extremely contentious boards that regard dissent as an obligation and treat no subject as undiscussable (Sonnenfeld 2002).

Since emotional intelligence is an important aspect of effective and healthy board dynamics, why do most boardrooms fail to incorporate it? This section ventures into the uncharted territories of these complexities, dissecting the nuanced intricacies and unveiling the subtle predicaments that arise when striving to apply EI in the boardroom. Through understanding these challenges, we seek not just to illuminate, but to provide a roadmap for harnessing the power of emotional intelligence to navigate the demanding landscape of the boardroom effectively and empathetically.

Embracing Feedback With Resilience

Most board members may find it challenging to receive feedback, particularly if they have transitioned from individual contributor roles where their expertise was rarely questioned. However, feedback is a crucial part of leadership development.

Feedback represents a core opportunity to learn and improve oneself, and those with strong emotional intelligence—particularly in areas such as empathy, reality testing, self-regard, and independence—can accept feedback without negatively impacting their self-perception. They use feedback as an opportunity for growth and improvement, and by considering diverse perspectives, board members can acquire a more in-depth understanding of their strengths and areas for improvement.

Emphasis on Rationality and Objectivity

The competitive and high-pressure nature of boardroom environments creates a culture that tends to prioritize rationality and objectivity over emotions. In these settings, the focus is often on making sound decisions based on facts, figures, and logical analysis, and as a result, emotional expressions or considerations may be seen as distractions or signs of weakness.

The pressure to maintain a composed and professional image can discourage the recognition and expression of emotions in the boardroom. Board members may feel compelled to hide their emotions, believing that showing vulnerability or sensitivity could undermine their credibility or authority. As a result, emotional intelligence, which involves understanding and managing emotions effectively, may be overshadowed or neglected.

This emphasis on logic and detached analysis can hinder the development of emotional intelligence skills among board members. Emotional intelligence encompasses competencies such as self-awareness, empathy, and relationship management, which are crucial for effective communication, conflict resolution, and relationship building. However, when emotions are undervalued or dismissed in the boardroom, directors may struggle to cultivate these skills, inhibiting their ability to navigate complex social dynamics and understand the impact of their emotions on decision-making processes.

Furthermore, the competitive nature of boardroom environments can create a sense of urgency and drive a "win at all costs" mentality. This can lead to a narrow focus on achieving outcomes, with little regard for the emotional well-being of individuals or the overall impact on relationships and team dynamics. Emotional intelligence requires a balance between achieving objectives and fostering positive relationships, but the pressure to prioritize results can overshadow the importance of emotional intelligence skills in the boardroom.

To address these challenges, there is a need to shift the narrative around emotions in the boardroom. Recognizing the value of emotions and their influence on decision-making processes can create a more inclusive and balanced environment. Encouraging open discussions about emotions, providing training and resources on emotional intelligence, and promoting a culture that values empathy and emotional well-being can help board members develop their emotional intelligence skills and create a healthier and more effective boardroom dynamic.

Ultimately, striking a balance between rationality and emotional intelligence can lead to more holistic and informed decision-making processes in the boardroom.

Underestimating Emotional Intelligence

Board members often lack a comprehensive understanding of emotional intelligence and its impact on organizational success. In many organizations, the focus is primarily on tangible outcomes and measurable results. Key performance indicators, financial metrics, and strategic goals often take precedence over what are considered "soft skills," which encompass the more intangible aspects of human interaction and emotional well-being. This limited understanding can lead board members to overlook the significance of EI and fail to prioritize its development within the boardroom.

Furthermore, the concept of emotional intelligence can be viewed as abstract and difficult to quantify. Unlike concrete metrics such as revenue growth or market share, the benefits of emotional intelligence are often indirect and nuanced. Directors may struggle to grasp how emotional intelligence can contribute to organizational success and thus may underestimate its value.

In addition, the corporate culture within the boardroom may reinforce a bias toward analytical thinking and rational decision-making. Directors, driven by a results-oriented mindset, may prioritize objective data and logical reasoning, considering emotions as subjective and unreliable factors in decision-making processes. This narrow perspective limits their recognition of emotional intelligence as a critical tool for effective leadership, collaboration, and relationship building.

To address this limited understanding of emotional intelligence, it is crucial to educate board members about its tangible benefits and impact on organizational success. Highlighting case studies and research that demonstrates how emotional intelligence enhances employee engagement, team effectiveness and overall business performance can help board members recognize its value.

Providing training and resources on emotional intelligence within the boardroom can also contribute to a deeper understanding and appreciation of its importance. Workshops, coaching sessions, or guest speakers can help board members develop their emotional intelligence skills and provide practical strategies for integrating emotional intelligence into boardroom practices.

Ultimately, recognizing emotional intelligence as a key driver of effective governance and organizational success can lead to more balanced and people-centric decision-making processes in the boardroom.

Overcoming Resistance to Emotional Expression in the Boardroom

Resistance to vulnerability and discomfort with expressing emotions can be prevalent in boardroom settings. The boardroom is often seen as a highly competitive and results-driven environment, where individuals strive to project an image of confidence and control. In this context, driven by the expectation to maintain a professional façade, board members may find it challenging to engage in open discussions about emotions and personal experiences. This reluctance to express vulnerability stems from the belief that emotions are best kept separate from professional interactions, and that acknowledging emotions may be seen as a sign of weakness or incompetence that could undermine one's credibility or authority.

Creating a safe space for emotional expression in the boardroom requires a shift in the organizational culture. It entails fostering an environment where vulnerability is seen as a strength rather than a weakness and where emotional honesty is valued. Board members need to feel that they can express their emotions without fear of judgment or negative repercussions.

Building trust among board members is crucial for overcoming resistance to vulnerability. When individuals feel secure and supported, they are more likely to open up and share their emotions.

Encouraging open and honest communication, active listening, and empathy can contribute to creating this safe space. Additionally, establishing clear expectations that emphasize the importance of emotional intelligence and emotional expression can help normalize these practices in the boardroom.

Leadership plays a critical role in setting the tone for emotional expression in the boardroom. Board chairs and executives can lead by example, demonstrating vulnerability and encouraging others to do the same. By sharing personal experiences and emotions, leaders create an atmosphere where others feel safe to express themselves.

Overcoming the resistance to vulnerability and discomfort with expressing emotions requires ongoing effort and commitment. However, by embracing vulnerability and emotional expression, board directors can foster deeper connections, enhance collaboration, and make more informed decisions for the benefit of the organization.

Complexity of Measuring Emotional Intelligence

Measuring and quantifying emotional intelligence can be a complex task. Unlike technical skills that can be assessed through certifications, qualifications, or standardized tests, emotional intelligence is more intangible and difficult to evaluate objectively. This presents challenges in tracking progress, setting benchmarks, and identifying specific areas for improvement in the realm of emotional intelligence.

One of the primary difficulties in measuring emotional intelligence lies in its multifaceted nature. EI encompasses a range of competencies, including self-awareness, self-regulation, empathy, and relationship management. These competencies are interconnected and dynamic, making it challenging to isolate and measure them individually through, for example, a simple numerical score.

Moreover, emotions themselves are highly subjective experiences. Each person may interpret and respond to emotions differently, which adds a layer of complexity to their measurement. Emotional responses can be influenced by various factors such as cultural background, personal experiences, and individual differences, making it challenging to develop standardized measures that apply universally.

Traditional assessment methods, such as self-report questionnaires or 360-degree feedback, are commonly used to evaluate emotional intelligence. However, these methods rely on individuals' self-perception or the perceptions of others, which may not always provide an accurate reflection of one's emotional intelligence capabilities. Self-report questionnaires, in particular, can be susceptible to biases and social desirability, as individuals may respond based on how they want to be perceived rather than their true emotional intelligence.

To address the complexities of measuring emotional intelligence, ongoing research and the development of robust assessment tools are essential. This involves the creation of reliable and valid measures that capture different aspects of emotional intelligence while accounting for individual and cultural differences. Incorporating multiple assessment methods—such as behavioral observations, performance-based tasks, ongoing practice, and feedback from peers and mentors—can provide a more comprehensive evaluation. Self-reflection is also beneficial, and while precise quantification may be difficult, individuals can still assess their growth by reflecting on their ability to recognize and regulate emotions, navigate social interactions, and manage conflicts effectively.

To address these challenges, it is crucial to raise awareness about the importance of emotional intelligence in the boardroom. Board members and leaders should be educated about the benefits of emotional intelligence, emphasizing its positive impact on decision-making, collaboration, and overall organizational success. Creating a supportive and inclusive boardroom culture that encourages emotional expression and vulnerability is essential.

Pursuing a Growth Mindset

Continuous learning is essential, especially in the ambiguous corporate landscape, as overestimating one's abilities can hinder personal and professional development. Board directors who acknowledge their areas for growth demonstrate humility and a willingness to learn. Emotional intelligence competencies such as self-regard, self-actualization, reality testing, and flexibility support board members in identifying opportunities for growth and embracing a growth mindset.

Proactive directors should engage in ongoing self-reflection to identify areas for improvement and strive for personal growth.

Besides, they should accept their own shortcomings and adopt a growth attitude by establishing self-respect and reality testing.

Harnessing the Power of Collective Intelligence

While once there was a tacit expectation that high-level professionals have all the answers, successful board members today value the ideas and input of a wider group of stakeholders. Embracing emotional intelligence skills like assertiveness, self-regard, flexibility, and interpersonal relationships empowers board members to foster a culture of collaboration, harnessing and complementing other directors' collective intelligence and perspectives.

Facilitating an open exchange of ideas provides a setting that promotes an efficient flow of information inside the boardroom. In closed and stressful settings like heated board meetings, it is vital to encourage open communication and mutual respect by modeling emotionally intelligent behaviors like empathy, self-regard, and positive interpersonal connections. Then, the entire board can combine its resources and pursue more creative ideas while making better, more well-informed decisions.

When decision-making incorporates a diverse range of perspectives, teamwork thrives, creativity flourishes, and superior choices emerge.

Embracing Active Listening

Listening is a cornerstone of effective governance, and board members who can truly listen to others demonstrate respect and foster a sense of belonging. As a high-level professional, it is important to always listen to other directors with an open mind and heart. Doing so requires showing empathy, being fully present in the moment, and wholeheartedly dedicating one's attention to the other person's perspective. Ignoring or pretending to listen can erode trust and lead to disengagement.

Emotional intelligence competencies such as empathy, interpersonal relationships, emotional expression, and flexibility enhance a director's capacity to listen actively, acknowledge input, and provide meaningful explanations for decisions. Board members who have developed these emotional intelligence competencies can better articulate complex ideas and offer viable direction for the organizations they are in.

Tackling Emotional Reactivity

Boards are corporate structures likely to concentrate a high proportion of individuals with strong personalities and powerful opinions. When faced with difficult situations that elicit an emotional response, effective board members employ a valuable emotional intelligence component: working to create new assumptions about the underlying dynamics at play. As a self-aware professional, this approach entails shifting away from personalizing the reactions and instead considering the possibility that team members may be experiencing burnout, causing even a minor additional task to feel overwhelming.

By challenging preconceived notions and embracing a fresh lens through which to perceive the situation, board members can gain deeper insights and devise more effective strategies for resolution. This approach helps them not only nurture empathy and understanding, but also embrace the opportunity to adapt their leadership style to better cater to the needs of their stakeholders.

Navigating Uncertainty and Stressful Scenarios

Volatility, uncertainty, chaos, and ambiguity (VUCA) have long been fundamental considerations in scenario planning as board directors anticipate unforeseen disruptions that may arise. However, in the present circumstances, individuals are consistently faced with an intensified manifestation of VUCA on a daily basis. The prevalence of uncertainty poses a significant test for directors, as planning and decision-making become more challenging due to the increased difficulty in predicting the future.

Since they are members of a cohesive organizational unit, board directors with high EI understand they do not have to navigate this uncertainty alone. When directors bring together diverse groups of individuals, they can tap into a collective intelligence that helps generate a broader range of ideas and perspectives. As such, they must maintain a rational mindset throughout decision-making, ensuring that decisions are not rushed or influenced by heightened emotions.

Unveiling the Dimensions of Corporate Reputation and the Role of Emotional Intelligence

> "It takes 20 years to build a reputation and five
> minutes to ruin it."
> — Warren Buffett

In the complex world of corporate reputation, a three-dimensional model can help in understanding its fundamental elements and their impact. These elements can be defined along three management axes, each crucial for shaping and maintaining both personal and organizational reputation. The three elements are: *time*, *business return*, and *agility*.

Time: Building Trust and Purpose

The X-axis represents *time*, where the trust a company has cultivated with stakeholders in the past resides. This trust is built upon consistently delivering on the company's stated vision and purpose. Organizations that align their actions with their core values earn repeat customers, loyalty from talented employees, long-term investors, and community support.

Considering the rapidly changing stakeholder dynamics, businesses have recognized the significance of ethical practices, compliance, governance, purpose, and sustainability as critical risk factors that shape long-term returns. Emotional intelligence promotes a strong ethical foundation, fostering stakeholder trust and credibility.

Source: Narayan (2020)

Business Return: Managing Risk and Expectations

The Y-axis represents *business return*, encompassing risk management and expectations management. Effectively managing risk is essential for maximizing opportunities and achieving superior returns. The ability to identify potential pitfalls, understand the necessary remedies, and execute proactive risk mitigation measures are crucial management expectations.

In today's dynamic business environment, resilience and adaptability are key. Emotional intelligence endows board members with the skills to navigate uncertainties, make informed decisions, and effectively manage expectations, thus strengthening the organization's reputation.

Agility: Integrated Response and Flexibility

The Z-axis represents *agility*, highlighting the importance of organizational integration. Companies must be agile and responsive to emerging challenges in an ever-changing world. The ability to harmonize diverse business functions and foster collaboration enables organizations to address issues swiftly and effectively.

Integrated teams facilitate informed decision-making, reducing vulnerability to market fluctuations and facilitating rapid adjustments in product and service offerings. Concepts such as the learning organization, empathy quotient, preemptive leadership, and fast-failing organizations all stem from the organization's flexibility to meet stakeholders' needs and consistently do what is right.

Emotional intelligence enhances interpersonal dynamics, promoting seamless collaboration and adaptability.

Deploying the Power of Stakeholder Engagement

Throughout all three dimensions, stakeholders play a pivotal role. Their engagement, management, and trust in the company's ability to succeed significantly shape its long-term prospects. In an era of heightened social media influence, a company's responsiveness and impactful actions are critical to business success. Well-prepared and well-integrated organizations are better positioned to address challenges and thrive in the long run.

UNECE (2022) officials concluded that, "a good reputation is something for which all industries, businesses and public service providers strive. Whether selling shoes or running hospitals, they rely on being known, liked and trusted." When considering the dynamics of time, business return and agility, one recognizes the intrinsic interconnectedness of these dimensions, which collectively form a seamless continuum.

By embracing emotional intelligence within these dimensions, organizations can cultivate trust, effectively manage risk, and drive agility. Hence, this cohesive, integrated approach enhances the company's reputation and fosters long-term success in a rapidly evolving business landscape. Organizations can truly thrive and secure their place as industry leaders through the harmonious interplay of these elements and the cultivation of emotional intelligence.

Exploring the Impact of Emotional Intelligence on Organizational Reputation

Devising a solid reputation that resonates positively with stakeholders is a prerequisite to success for any enterprise. Every interaction, every decision, and every aspect of an organization's operations contributes to the delicate tapestry that forms its reputation. As defined by Fombrun et al. (2000), an organization's reputation reflects its relative position, internally among employees and externally among customers and other stakeholders. In a world brimming with choices, a positive reputation becomes the lifeline that sets businesses apart from the competition.

Reputation-building is not a one-time endeavor but an ongoing commitment. It requires consistent efforts to meet and exceed expectations, to listen attentively to feedback, and to adapt swiftly to changing circumstances. In this context, emotional intelligence—encompassing self-awareness, empathy, and effective communication—is crucial in shaping positive perceptions and cultivating strong stakeholder relationships. Every interaction becomes an opportunity to shape perceptions and leave a lasting impression. Since reputation is a key buffer for resilience, organizations need to be more proactive in managing it for the long term. Infusing business decision-making and operations with emotional intelligence constitutes one of the key avenues to building this long-term reputational resilience.

Ethical conduct, ethical business practices, and overall ethical decision-making are paramount for organizations. Any lapse in these areas can result in severe reputational damage. When an organization fails to uphold ethical standards, it risks losing the trust and confidence of its stakeholders, including customers, employees, investors, and the wider community. Negative publicity, public backlash, and legal repercussions can follow, leading to significant harm to the organization's reputation.

The Advantages of a Strong Organizational Reputation

Industries and businesses strive to carve a niche for themselves by nurturing a reputation that embodies integrity, quality, and reliability. It becomes a badge of honor; a testament to their commitment to excellence. Thus, having a positive reputation instills customer confidence, fostering loyalty and encouraging repeat business. A firm's reputation constitutes 63% of its market value, and 58% of top executives recognize the significance of managing that reputation online, according to Gitnux (2023).

A favorable organizational reputation offers numerous benefits that contribute to the long-term success and sustainability of a company. These benefits include:

Risk mitigation: When directors take into account the potential ethical implications of their decisions, they can avoid actions that might lead to negative publicity or damage to the organization's reputation. By consistently making ethical choices, organizations can maintain a positive reputation, which is crucial for building trust with stakeholders and attracting customers, partners, and investors.

Attracting top talent: A positive reputation for ethical conduct and sound business practices enhances an organization's attractiveness as an employer. Talented individuals are drawn to organizations that prioritize ethics as they seek alignment between their personal values and those of the organization they work for.

Stronger customer relationships: Having a strong reputation brings a broader range of perspectives into the organization, fostering trust among different communities. Ethical conduct and transparent business practices demonstrate a genuine commitment to meeting customer needs while considering broader societal and environmental impacts.

Enhancing trust and transparency: Most of the time, openness regarding business practices and operations represents a viable test for the board's overall transparency and trustworthiness. Even if an organization's track record in this area is not flawless, being transparent about the challenges and efforts represents an essential component in the overall success of a company.

Enhanced brand image: A positive reputation enhances the perception of the organization's brand in the eyes of customers, clients, and stakeholders. It builds trust, credibility, and loyalty, which can lead to increased customer retention and acquisition. Ultimately, a strong brand image resulting from a good reputation contributes to the long-term success and growth of the organization.

Stronger financial performance: Stronger financial performance is a significant benefit that stems from having a good reputation. A positive reputation helps build trust and credibility among customers, investors, and other stakeholders. This trust translates into increased customer loyalty, higher customer satisfaction, and improved brand perception, which ultimately drives revenue growth.

Furthermore, a good reputation can attract investors, who view the organization as a reliable and stable investment opportunity. This can result in increased access to capital, lower borrowing costs, and improved financial stability. Strong financial performance allows the organization to invest in innovation, expand operations, and seize new opportunities.

The Consequences of an Impaired Organizational Reputation

Since approximately 70% to 80% of market value is derived from intangible assets that are difficult to evaluate—such as brand equity, intellectual capital, and goodwill—organizations face heightened vulnerability to any factors that can harm their reputations, as outlined by Eccles, Newquist, and Schatz (2007). Maintaining a long-term commitment to ethics and ethical business practices is essential for safeguarding a positive reputation and ensuring the long-term success and sustainability of the organization.

Poor reputation can cause significant damage to an organization in the following ways:

Loss of trust: A poor reputation erodes trust in the organization among various stakeholders, including customers, employees, investors, and partners.

Deterring talent: Talent attraction becomes challenging when potential candidates perceive an organization's approach to business operations and overall ethics as hindering their personal growth. Existing employees may also lose faith in their advancement opportunities and seek employment elsewhere.

Customer disengagement: A weak reputation hindered by questionable corporate practices poses the risk of losing customers to competitors who prioritize these values. In some cases, certain groups may even boycott a business, further impacting its market share.

Investor scrutiny: Shareholders are increasingly concerned about factors that impact an organization's reputation and, consequently, the value of their investments. As a result, they are demanding more information and transparency regarding business conduct and organizational impact on the society and the environment.

Legal and regulatory penalties: A poor reputation can invite increased scrutiny from regulatory bodies, leading to legal and compliance issues. Negative publicity and public perception can trigger investigations, audits, and potential legal consequences, resulting in financial penalties, lawsuits, and damaged relationships with regulatory authorities.

Financial implications: A damaged reputation can have direct financial implications. Negative publicity can lead to reduced revenues, increased marketing, and public relations costs to repair the reputation and decreased shareholder value. Additionally, borrowing costs may increase as lenders perceive greater risk associated with the organization's poor reputation.

Emotional intelligence is pivotal in shaping and maintaining a positive reputation for ethical business practices. As Robert Noyce once said, "If ethics are poor at the top, that behavior is copied down through the organization."

Emotionally intelligent board members have the capacity to better navigate the challenges and complexities of fostering an ethical corporate culture, which is then reflected in the overall organizational reputation. This can be done in the following ways:

Cultivating inclusive leadership: Emotional intelligence enables board directors to cultivate inclusive leadership styles characterized by empathy, understanding, and adaptability. These qualities contribute to creating an organizational culture that embraces a strong commitment to ethics and respect for the environment and society, including the perspectives of all individuals.

Effective stakeholder engagement: In most instances, board members with emotional intelligence can engage with stakeholders to foster trust and demonstrate a genuine commitment to ethical decision-making. They can navigate difficult conversations, address concerns, and actively listen to feedback, strengthening relationships and reputation.

Conflict resolution and decision-making: As already emphasized in earlier sections of the book, emotional intelligence allows board members to effectively manage conflicts and difficult business decisions. By considering diverse perspectives, recognizing biases, and making inclusive decisions, directors can mitigate reputational risks and foster an environment of respect and understanding.

Worksheet: EI and Organizational Reputation

Reflect on each question and provide thoughtful responses. Consider real-life scenarios or hypothetical situations to deepen your understanding.

1. Reflect on a situation where you observed or experienced a high level of emotional intelligence within an organization. How did it positively impact the organization's reputation? Provide specific examples if possible.

2. Identify and describe specific EI competencies or behaviors that can contribute to a positive organizational reputation (e.g., empathy, effective communication, conflict resolution).

3. Consider a situation where a lack of emotional intelligence negatively affected an organization's reputation. What were the consequences? How did it impact stakeholders' perceptions of the organization?

4. Reflect on the role of leadership in promoting and cultivating emotional intelligence within an organization. How does leadership behavior and EI influence the organization's reputation?

5. In your opinion, which stakeholders are most influenced by an organization's emotional intelligence? Why do you think they are particularly sensitive to EI?

6. Reflect on any personal experiences where you have

witnessed or experienced the impact of emotional intelligence on an organization's reputation. What lessons did you learn from those experiences?

Exploring the Future of EI in Board Leadership

As the landscape of board leadership continues to evolve, the role of emotional intelligence is gaining prominence. Traditionally, board leadership has emphasized analytical and strategic thinking, but the future calls for a greater emphasis on emotional intelligence.

Emotional intelligence is essential for effective board leadership for several reasons. First, board members must navigate complex interpersonal dynamics, both within the boardroom and with key stakeholders. Emotional intelligence enables directors to navigate conflicts, build consensus and foster a positive board culture. Second, emotional intelligence enhances decision-making by considering intuitive and logical analysis, as well as the impact of decisions on individuals and the organization as a whole. Third, it fosters strong relationships and effective communication among board members, promoting collaboration and trust.

Managing economic uncertainty and market downturns requires a delicate balancing act for board directors. From economic challenges to internal hierarchies, directors can rely on emotional intelligence to navigate these challenges while nurturing team morale and increasing productivity.

Changing Dynamics Between the Board and Upper Management

Given the operational and financial problems and fiduciary responsibilities, the board and executive leadership relationship will face increasing pressures as directors attempt to become more active in company activities. To maintain the appropriate balance between governance and management and to promote their crucial collaborative relationship, directors and executives will be urged to mutually reaffirm their respective roles, duties, and lines of authority.

Integrating More Diversity of Perspectives

Companies are increasingly realizing that diverse boards bring broader perspectives, experiences, and insights, leading to better decision-making and improved organizational performance.

In early May 2023, the latest board diversity index was released by the Governance Institute in collaboration with Watermark Search International. It showcased concerning findings regarding cultural, ethnic, and gender diversity on boards. In Australia, there is a lack of progress in achieving cultural and ethnic diversity, with 90% of board members coming from an Anglo-Celtic background, consistent with previous reports. In addition, the concentration of female directors is worrisome, with just 19% of current female directors holding a significant 48% of all female-held board seats. Nonetheless, the report predicts positive strides in achieving gender parity by 2030, based on current trends.

Diversity in the boardroom brings together individuals with different backgrounds, perspectives, and cognitive styles. Board directors with high EI are capable of creating an environment where diverse voices are heard and decisions are made through a collaborative and inclusive process, leading to more robust and well-rounded outcomes.

Leading with Vulnerability and Transparency

Without a doubt, the boardroom is a dynamic environment driven by high stakes, where struggles involving ego, power, rules, and authority constantly emerge. Amidst the complex dynamics of group interactions, it is not always clear how board directors should react and relate to one another.

Board members who have the capacity to embrace vulnerability and transparency in their communication can build trust and foster a more positive boardroom culture. By openly addressing economic challenges, sharing honest updates, and inviting team input, directors can create an environment where everyone feels valued, engaged, and empowered to contribute to their solutions.

Encouraging Cross-Cultural Leadership

Global leaders, including board members, must adapt their leadership styles to meet different cultures' diverse needs and expectations. Emotional intelligence empowers directors to be flexible, adjusting their approach to effectively inspire and motivate teams across borders. As such, the traditional archetype of a successful global leader is evolving. While intelligence, business acumen, and the ability to manage operations remain essential, cultural sensitivity and emotional intelligence are now recognized as critical attributes for driving international success. The ability to understand and navigate cultural nuances, along with the capacity to build strong relationships across diverse environments, is becoming the trump card for effective global leadership.

Creating Psychological Safety

Building a psychologically safe work environment becomes even more critical in uncertain times. Emotional intelligence enables board members to foster a culture of psychological safety, where all members feel comfortable expressing their opinions, ideas, and concerns without fear of judgment or reprisal, resulting in innovation, collaboration, and inclusivity.

Embracing AI and Technological Advancements

Artificial intelligence is one of the most significant disruptions (if not the biggest disruption) of our times. Thus, directors must embrace new technologies while considering their impact on society and business. Emotional intelligence helps directors to navigate the challenges associated with AI, such as job displacement and ethical considerations. By combining technical know-how with strategic thinking and empathy, directors can effectively harness AI's potential while ensuring the well-being and growth of their organizations.

Long-Term Strategy and Sustainability

Emotional intelligence can assist boards in developing long-term strategies that consider not only financial performance but also the social and environmental impact of the organization. By incorporating empathy and understanding into their strategic planning, boards can navigate ethical dilemmas, anticipate stakeholder concerns, and make choices that align with the organization's long-term sustainability goals. Emotional intelligence also enhances their ability to communicate and champion sustainability initiatives within the organization, driving positive change and responsible practices.

Stakeholder Engagement

Stakeholder engagement is no longer limited to shareholders alone; it encompasses a wide range of individuals and groups, including employees, customers, communities, and regulatory bodies. Boards must now consider the perspectives and concerns of these stakeholders and proactively engage with them to build trust and foster mutually beneficial relationships.

Emotional intelligence equips board leaders with the ability to understand and empathize with stakeholders' needs and interests. By putting themselves in the shoes of stakeholders, board leaders can make informed decisions that consider the broader impact on all involved parties. This empathetic approach fosters trust, strengthens relationships, and enhances the board's ability to navigate complex stakeholder dynamics.

Looking ahead, the future of EI in board leadership lies in its integration as a core competency for stakeholder engagement. Boards can prioritize emotional intelligence by fostering a culture of empathy, communication, and collaboration. They can invest in board education and development programs that focus on emotional intelligence skills, enabling board leaders to navigate the complexities of stakeholder engagement effectively.

Ethical Decision-Making

In an era where ethical considerations hold increasing importance, emotional intelligence is emerging as a critical factor in board leadership for ethical decision-making. The future of board leadership lies in the integration of EI competencies that enable directors to navigate complex ethical dilemmas and uphold the highest standards of integrity and accountability.

Ethical decision-making requires a deep understanding of one's values, the ability to assess moral implications, and the courage to act in accordance with ethical principles. Emotional intelligence plays a pivotal role in this process by fostering self-awareness and aligning personal values with ethical conduct. Directors with high EI can identify their own biases, examine potential conflicts of interest, and make ethical decisions that prioritize the interests of all stakeholders.

Emotional intelligence training can help board members navigate complex ethical dilemmas and ensure decisions align with ethical principles and organizational values.

Leadership Succession

Leadership succession is a crucial aspect of board governance, and the future of board leadership lies in integrating emotional intelligence as a fundamental factor in leadership succession planning and implementation.

Emotional intelligence plays a key role in identifying and developing potential leaders, such as future board chairs and CEOs, within the organization. Boards that prioritize EI in their succession planning process can assess individuals not only based on their technical skills and experience, but also their ability to navigate complex social dynamics, build relationships, and inspire others. By evaluating emotional intelligence alongside traditional leadership attributes, boards can identify candidates who possess the interpersonal skills and self-awareness required to lead effectively.

Furthermore, emotional intelligence facilitates effective leadership development and mentoring programs. Boards can invest in the development of emotional intelligence competencies among potential successors, equipping them with the necessary skills to navigate challenges, manage teams, and make sound decisions. This focus on emotional intelligence ensures that future leaders are not only technically proficient but also possess the empathy and emotional resilience required for effective leadership.

Board Effectiveness

In the realm of board leadership, the future holds great promise for the integration of emotional intelligence as a catalyst for enhancing board effectiveness. Boards that prioritize and cultivate EI competencies among their members—through regular emotional intelligence assessments, self-reflection exercises, and coaching— can foster a collaborative and high-performing environment, leading to more impactful decision-making, improved governance, and ultimately, better organizational outcomes.

Investing in Personal and Professional Development

Indeed, the future of EI in board leadership may involve a focus on continuous learning and adaptability. Board members can engage in ongoing development initiatives, stay updated with emerging research and best practices, and adapt their leadership styles to navigate changing business landscapes and societal expectations. Emotional intelligence, stress management, and self-reflection are key areas to focus on to enhance their personal and professional growth. By investing in coaching and continuous development, directors can strengthen their emotional intelligence, decision-making abilities, and resilience to thrive in challenging times.

As the landscape of board leadership evolves, emotional intelligence will become increasingly critical for effective governance. The future of board leadership lies in recognizing and embracing the value of emotional intelligence in navigating complex interpersonal dynamics, enhancing decision-making, fostering strong relationships, and engaging with stakeholders. Prioritizing and developing emotional intelligence among board members, helps organizations position themselves for sustainable success in the ever-changing business landscape.

Worksheet: The Future of EI in Board Leadership

Reflect on each question and provide thoughtful responses. Consider real-life scenarios or hypothetical situations to deepen your understanding.

1. Consider the potential benefits of incorporating emotional intelligence into board leadership. How might it enhance decision-making, board dynamics, and overall governance?

2. Reflect on any challenges or barriers that may hinder the adoption of emotional intelligence in board leadership. What factors might contribute to resistance or reluctance?

3. Explore emerging trends and advancements in the field of emotional intelligence. How might these advancements shape the future of emotional intelligence in board leadership?

4. Consider the role of technology in enhancing emotional intelligence in the boardroom. How can technology be leveraged to support and develop emotional intelligence skills among board members?

5. Reflect on the ethical considerations associated with emotional intelligence in board leadership. How can emotional intelligence be leveraged responsibly and ethically in decision-making processes?

6. Imagine a future scenario where emotional intelligence is a core competency for board members. How would this impact

board effectiveness, stakeholder relationships, and overall governance?

7. What steps can individuals and organizations take to promote and prioritize emotional intelligence in board leadership?

Strategic Recruitment and Succession Planning by Integrating EI

While a track record of successful performance and expertise in building and shaping businesses across borders remains important, there is now a growing recognition that cultural competency and emotional intelligence are crucial differentiators for effective international leaders. As such, board-level recruitment and succession planning dynamics have significantly transformed.

The evolving landscape of shareholder and consumer expectations drives a transformative shift in board oversight and practices, as revealed by PwC's 2022 Annual Corporate Directors Survey of over 700 public company directors. This shift arises as a direct response to the heightened demands placed upon boards to adapt and meet stakeholders' evolving needs and expectations.

According to a comprehensive study conducted by Ownership Matters, it has been revealed that Australia's leading 300 listed companies have been sluggish in recruiting new talent for their boardrooms. Besides, directors rarely face repercussions for the poor returns experienced by shareholders, solidifying the perception that these top boards operate as exclusive "invitation-only" clubs. The study analyzed nearly 6,000 directorships across ASX 300 companies over a 15-year period. One of the most notable findings was the slow rate of director turnover, averaging only 12.75% during this timeframe.

Likewise, boards of underperforming companies refresh their

membership at a rate only slightly higher than boards of other companies (Shapiro 2020).

> "People who demand neutrality in any situation
> are usually not neutral but in favor
> of the status quo."
> — Max Eastman

Given the opacity surrounding the election of board member positions, transparency and diversity are lacking. Securing a position within an ASX 100 board still heavily relies on personal connections and networks. It is paramount to acknowledge and accept that this is a reality, while also actively working towards correcting it.

Uncovering the Facets of Strategic Recruitment

Strategic recruitment is an all-encompassing strategy for finding, attracting, and hiring top individuals for a company. Based on the work of talent management expert Dr. John Sullivan, strategic recruiting relies on three pillars: recruitment-directed marketing, employer branding, and skilled selling.

Marketing-focused recruitment: To draw in top talent effectively, organizations must employ a marketing mindset in their recruitment efforts. This involves identifying candidates and employing targeted marketing strategies to engage and attract them. By understanding the requirements and preferences of prospective candidates, organizations can customize their recruitment messages and channels to captivate their attention and interest.

Employer branding: A robust employer brand is essential for attracting and retaining top talent. It involves shaping and promoting the organization's reputation as an employer of choice. This includes emphasizing the company's values, culture, employee benefits, career development opportunities, and positive work environment. Through internal and external communication that is consistent and genuine, organizations can cultivate an employer brand that resonates with prospective candidates and sets them apart from other businesses.

Skilled selling: In strategic recruiting, organizations must take a proactive and persuasive approach to present the opportunity to prospective candidates. To attract high-potential prospects to join an organization, skilled selling requires effectively articulating the value proposition of the organization and the specific role for their career development, and presenting a compelling case for why the organization is the best option.

The board recruitment process is a critical aspect of building an effective and diverse board of directors. Ideally, it should involve several steps aimed at identifying, evaluating, and selecting candidates who possess the necessary skills, experience, and attributes to contribute to the organization's governance and strategic direction.

The first step is to conduct a thorough assessment of the board's current composition and identify any gaps or areas of expertise that need to be filled. This helps in defining the desired qualifications, skills, and attributes for potential board members.

Organizations may employ various methods to identify potential board candidates. This can include engaging search firms, utilizing online platforms, or reaching out to professional associations and networks. The goal is to create a pool of diverse and qualified candidates.

Once potential candidates are identified, a comprehensive evaluation process is conducted. This typically involves reviewing their resumes; assessing their qualifications, experience, and accomplishments; and conducting interviews.

Shortlisted candidates are typically invited for board interviews. These interviews provide an opportunity to assess the candidates' alignment with the organization's values; their understanding of the organization's mission, vision, and strategy; as well as their ability to contribute effectively to board discussions and decision-making.

After evaluating the candidates, the board makes a selection based on a combination of factors, including qualifications, expertise, diversity, and cultural fit. The decision is typically made through reaching a consensus via a board vote. Background and reference checks, including verifying credentials and conducting due diligence also take place at this stage.

Once selected, new board members undergo an onboarding and orientation process to familiarize themselves with the organization, its governance structure, policies, procedures, and strategic priorities. This includes providing them with relevant materials, introducing them to key stakeholders, and providing mentorship or buddy systems to facilitate a smooth transition.

Effective board recruitment is an ongoing process. Boards should regularly assess their composition, identify areas for improvement, and proactively seek opportunities to enhance diversity, skills, and expertise. This may involve implementing term limits, establishing board development programs, or engaging in board succession planning.

It is important for organizations to ensure transparency, fairness, and diversity throughout the board recruitment process. By implementing a robust and inclusive recruitment process, organizations can build a high-performing board that brings diverse perspectives, experiences, and expertise to the table, leading to effective governance and strategic decision-making.

Shifting Priorities in the Recruitment Process

The general recruitment process for board members is undergoing significant changes as organizations seek to enhance their governance practices and adapt to evolving business environments. Boards play a crucial role in decision-making and strategic guidance, and now recognizing the need for diverse perspectives, expertise, and leadership qualities, organizations are prioritizing differently in the board recruitment process.

While technical competencies have traditionally been the primary focus of board recruitment, organizations are placing increased importance on leadership qualities and boardroom dynamics. This includes assessing candidates' ability to contribute effectively to board discussions, challenge conventional thinking, foster constructive debate, and work collaboratively with fellow board members and management. Emotional intelligence, strong communication skills, adaptability, and a willingness to embrace diversity of thought are valued attributes.

The emphasis is also expanding to include cultural sensitivity and awareness. Cultural competency plays a vital role in navigating diverse environments and fostering meaningful connections with stakeholders from different backgrounds. Merging or acquiring businesses in different countries requires leaders to navigate unique cultural dynamics. Whether it is a family-run business in India or a company in Bosnia, successful leadership engagement hinges on cultural awareness and the ability to adapt approaches based on local expectations and norms. Leaders with cultural competency possess the empathy needed to observe and understand what is effective, what is not, and what is expected within a specific cultural context. This awareness allows them to make informed decisions and develop strong working relationships with individuals from different cultures.

As the Muttard Foundation outlines, "Recruiting, developing, and retaining appropriate individuals to serve in board roles is a difficult and time-consuming job. Healthy organizations are willing to make a major investment of time and effort in these activities to build a strong organization" (Miloff 2017).

In addition to solid organizational groundwork, successful board recruiting efforts also need emotional intelligence to provide a constructive and welcoming environment for all candidates. Directors may build trust, strengthen relationships, and guarantee a diverse and active board by using the concepts of emotional intelligence.

With the growing focus on sustainability and corporate social responsibility, organizations are prioritizing environment, social, and governance (ESG) competence in board recruitment. Boards are expected to understand and oversee ESG risks, opportunities, and strategies, and as a result, candidates with expertise in sustainability, climate change, social impact, ethical governance, and responsible business practices are in high demand.

Emotional intelligence in cultivating connections with stakeholders outside the organization is crucial to increasing visibility and influence. This can help navigate complex stakeholder dynamics, forge partnerships, and ultimately contribute to the long-term success and sustainability of the organization.

When new members join the board, it becomes a shared responsibility of both the board and the executive leadership team to set a positive tone. This includes clearly communicating the purpose and mission of the organization and providing thorough induction and training to ensure that the new members have a comprehensive understanding of their roles and responsibilities. By doing so, the board and executive leadership team create a solid foundation for the new members to contribute effectively, align with the organization's objectives, and make informed decisions in line with their designated roles.

In addition, emotionally intelligent directors can provide more effective mentoring and onboarding for new directors. Thus, they can anticipate and understand the challenges faced by new directors, providing support that is sensitive to their emotional journey during the transition.

Furthermore, boards must allocate sufficient time for robust succession planning discussions. They must recognize the importance of regular refreshment and succession planning (i.e. identifying and nurturing potential future board leaders) to ensure continuity and adaptability.

According to Diligent (2019):

> A policy for a board succession planning outlines the process that boards and committees need to use for planning to replace board members, a board chair and executive directors, either because of an existing vacancy or to plan for the future vacancy of a position.

It ultimately falls upon the board chair or leads to prioritize board succession planning and have candid conversations with fellow board members when necessary. Leveraging emotional intelligence skills like empathy, self-awareness, and conflict resolution, board leaders can navigate these discussions effectively, ensuring the board is equipped with the right mix of skills and expertise to guide the organization successfully.

When businesses actively seek out and engage with members of underrepresented populations, diverse board candidates that may bring fresh perspectives to an organization can be found. Structured interviews, blind evaluations, and various interview panels combat unconscious bias and assure fair assessments based on merit and potential, which are essential in recruiting. These methods encourage a more varied and representative board, which benefits from increased insight and decision-making efficiency.

In the long run, a cohesive board that values emotional intelligence can foster a culture that is more resilient to change, thus making leadership transitions smoother and less disruptive. The enhanced insight and decision-making efficiency driven by emotional intelligence can be the catalyst to transform board succession, reducing leadership failures and ultimately enhancing organizational performance.

The board should also consider CEO succession planning. With only 35% of organizations having a formalized succession planning process for critical roles (Associated for Talent Development 2019), there is a significant gap in ensuring a smooth leadership transition. In this vein, McKinsey (2017) highlights that over 74% of leaders feel unprepared and lack the necessary training to tackle the challenges they encounter, further exacerbating the issue. Furthermore, the high percentage failure rate of 60% for executives within the first 18 months of promotion or hire highlights the importance of proper onboarding and support to set leaders up for success.

Strategy-Business (2015) revealed that companies experiencing forced succession could have generated a staggering $112 billion more in market value if they had implemented better succession planning strategies. Furthermore, the same study found that companies in the lowest performance quartile tend to have inadequate succession practices, resulting in a higher frequency of CEO turnover compared to companies in higher quartiles.

Including emotional intelligence in board succession planning can be achieved through various strategies. For example, organizations can engage external consultants who can provide EI assessment tools and interview processes that specifically evaluate emotional intelligence competencies alongside technical qualifications. They can also provide training and development opportunities to enhance emotional intelligence skills for new and existing board members.

By considering emotional intelligence during the succession planning process, organizations can ensure that incoming board members possess the necessary competencies to effectively lead and contribute to the board's overall effectiveness.

Devising a Comprehensive Board Skills Matrix

A board skills matrix is a valuable tool for assessing and mapping the skills and expertise of board directors. It provides a structured framework for evaluating the collective capabilities of the board and identifying any gaps or areas for development, since a well-balanced board enhances a company's performance and decision-making. When developing a skills matrix, it is crucial to take into account the organization's strategic objectives and identify the skills necessary to support the achievement of those objectives.

One of the primary benefits of a comprehensive board skills matrix is improved board effectiveness. Research by Kiel and Nicholson (2003) suggests that board composition, including skills and expertise, has a significant impact on board effectiveness and decision-making. A well-designed skills matrix ensures that the board has the necessary expertise to address critical issues, such as financial management, industry knowledge, legal compliance, and risk assessment.

In addition, a board skills matrix promotes transparency and accountability in corporate governance. Sundaramurthy and Lewis (2003) identify transparency as a key factor in board decision-making processes. By clearly documenting the skills and qualifications of board members, the board skills matrix provides stakeholders with insight into the board's capabilities and expertise. This transparency fosters trust and confidence among shareholders, investors, and other stakeholders.

A skills matrix aids in succession planning and board refreshment. Ongoing board renewal ensures long-term organizational performance. By identifying skills gaps and areas for development, the board skills matrix helps guide board succession planning efforts, ensuring a pipeline of directors with the necessary skills and experience to lead the organization in the future.

Moreover, a comprehensive skills matrix supports board diversity and inclusion. Adams, Hermalin, and Weisbach (2010) suggest that diverse boards are associated with better corporate performance. The skills matrix helps identify diversity gaps and promotes the inclusion of directors with diverse backgrounds, perspectives, and expertise, which enriches board discussions and decision-making processes.

The skills matrix is typically presented in a tabular format. OnBoard (2022) describes the board skills matrix as, "a grid that lists board members (or potential members) along one axis and necessary skills along the other axis. The two are cross-checked to map which directors possess various skills, usually marked with an 'X' or checkmark."

Usually, a standard board matrix assesses the subsequent aspects:

- Industry background

- C-suite title

- Risk management

- Strategic expertise

- Marketing acumen

- Revenue operations proficiency

- Technological savviness

- Governance understanding

- Additional resources

- Network connections

Example of a Board Skills Matrix

Board Skills Matrix

The Board skills matrix below represents some of the key skills that our Board has identified as particularly valuable to the effective oversight of the Company and the execution of our strategy. This matrix highlights the depth and breadth of skills on the Board.

Experience, Expertise or Attribute	Daleo	Driver	Feidler	Hough	Humann	Marcus	Marshall	McKinley	Smith	Stock	Templeton
General Management & Business Operations	✔	✔	✔	✔	✔	✔	✔	✔	✔	✔	✔
CEO Experience					✔	✔			✔		✔
CFO Experience	✔					✔					
CTO Experience								✔	✔		
EFX Industry Knowledge	✔				✔			✔	✔		✔
Technology	✔		✔			✔		✔	✔		✔
Finance/Financial Industry	✔	✔	✔	✔	✔	✔	✔	✔	✔	✔	✔
Accounting	✔		✔	✔	✔	✔			✔		
Risk Management	✔	✔	✔	✔	✔	✔	✔	✔	✔		✔
International Business	✔	✔	✔	✔			✔	✔	✔	✔	✔
Strategy Development	✔	✔	✔		✔	✔	✔	✔	✔	✔	✔
Mergers & Acquisitions	✔	✔	✔		✔	✔	✔		✔	✔	✔
Consumer Marketing		✔	✔		✔	✔	✔		✔	✔	✔
Legal/Regulatory		✔	✔			✔	✔		✔		
Corporate Governance		✔		✔	✔	✔	✔		✔	✔	✔

Source: Equilar (2017)

As can be seen in the example above, a skills matrix typically focuses on technical competencies and industry knowledge. However, recognizing the significance of emotional intelligence in effective leadership and decision-making, it is proposed that there is a need to integrate emotional intelligence into the board skills matrix.

Goleman, Boyatzis, and McKee (2013) suggest that leaders with high emotional intelligence have a greater ability to navigate complex interpersonal dynamics, inspire and motivate others, and make sound decisions. Therefore, including EI as a criterion in the board skills matrix helps ensure that board directors possess the essential skills to lead and govern effectively.

One of the key benefits of incorporating emotional intelligence into the board skills matrix is improved board dynamics and collaboration. This is supported by Jordan and Troth (2004), who discovered a positive relationship between emotional intelligence and teamwork. By assessing directors' emotional intelligence, the board can identify individuals who are skilled at managing their own emotions, and understanding and empathizing with the emotions of others. This fosters a more harmonious and collaborative boardroom environment, enhancing communication, problem-solving, and decision-making processes.

Additionally, incorporating emotional intelligence into the skills matrix enhances board effectiveness. Directors with high emotional intelligence are better equipped to handle conflicts, manage stress, and build relationships, which are essential for effective board functioning (Côté and Miners 2006). By recognizing emotional intelligence as a vital competency, the board can ensure that its directors possess the essential interpersonal and self-management skills needed for effective governance.

Moreover, integrating emotional intelligence into the skills matrix supports stakeholder engagement and satisfaction. According to Boyatzis et al. (2015) leaders with higher emotional intelligence are more likely to establish meaningful connections with stakeholders, leading to increased trust, loyalty, and positive organizational outcomes. Including emotional intelligence as a criterion helps the board select directors who are capable of understanding and addressing the diverse needs and perspectives of stakeholders, enhancing overall stakeholder satisfaction and trust in the organization's leadership.

Board recruitment presents a complex undertaking that requires careful attention and consideration. Selecting a board director is a multifaceted process. Presented below are various factors to consider when choosing and assessing board directors:

- **Cultural awareness:** Assess their ability to navigate cultural differences, adapt to various business environments, and demonstrate inclusive behaviors.

- **Emotional awareness:** Gauge the candidate's self-awareness of their own emotions, as well as their ability to recognize and understand the emotions of others.

- **Conflict resolution:** Evaluate their proficiency in managing conflicts constructively. Look for evidence of their ability to listen actively, seek common ground, and facilitate collaborative problem-solving.

- **Ethical awareness:** Assess the candidate's understanding and commitment to ethical principles, as well as their awareness of and concern for environmental and societal issues.

- **Empathy:** Analyze their ability to consider different perspectives, demonstrate compassion, and build relationships based on trust and understanding.

- **Listening skills:** Observe how they engage with other professionals, assessing their inclination to consider diverse perspectives and contemplate alternative viewpoints.

Incorporating emotional intelligence into a board skills matrix brings valuable advantages to corporate governance. This integration ensures that board directors possess the necessary emotional and interpersonal competencies to navigate complex challenges, inspire others, and make sound decisions. As research indicates, emotional intelligence is a critical component of effective leadership and should be recognized and considered in the selection and evaluation of board directors.

Worksheet: Strategic Board Recruitment and EI

Reflect on each question and provide thoughtful responses. Consider real-life scenarios or hypothetical situations to deepen your understanding.

1. Reflect on the current board composition in your organization (or a hypothetical organization). Do you believe emotional intelligence is adequately considered in the recruitment and selection of board members? Why or why not?

2. Reflect on the qualities or skills associated with emotional intelligence that would be valuable in board members. List some specific EI competencies that you believe are important for effective board leadership.

3. Explore potential barriers or challenges in integrating emotional intelligence into board recruitment and succession planning. What factors might hinder the consideration of EI in these processes?

4. Consider the role of emotional intelligence in effective succession planning. How can EI be integrated into the identification, evaluation, and development of potential board successors?

5. Explore strategies to integrate emotional intelligence into board recruitment and succession planning. How can organizations actively assess and evaluate EI competencies in potential board members?

6. Consider the potential risks or limitations of solely focusing on emotional intelligence in board recruitment. How can these limitations be mitigated or balanced with other critical competencies and qualifications?

Chapter 4

REDEFINING GOVERNANCE: A HEART-DRIVEN BOARD FOR THE 21ST CENTURY

Understanding the Heart-Driven Board

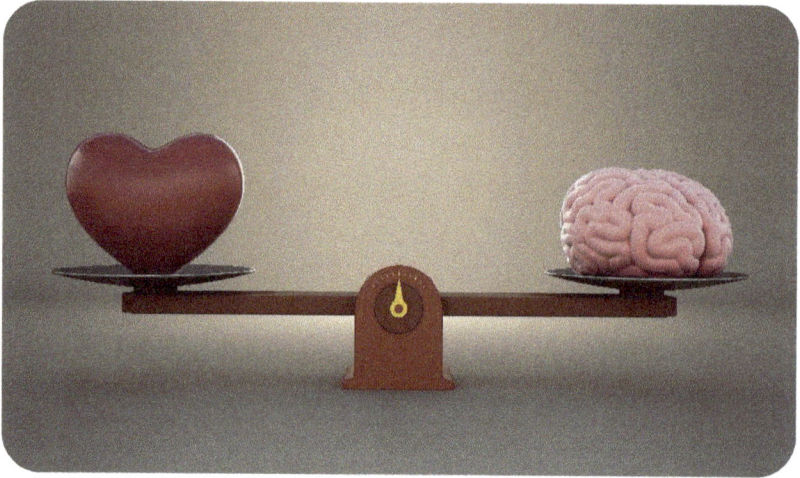

In the fast-paced and complex landscape of the 21st century, the traditional model of governance is being challenged. Organizations and institutions are recognizing the need for a transformative approach to leadership and corporate governance—one that goes beyond conventional strategies and embraces a heart-driven paradigm.

The concept of a heart-driven board is gaining momentum as a catalyst for positive change, redefining the role of boards in driving innovation, fostering ethical decision-making, and creating a more sustainable and compassionate world.

A heart-driven board is characterized by a deep commitment to values, ethics, and social responsibility. It is a collective of individuals who understand the importance of listening to their intuition, connecting with their emotions, and cultivating empathy and compassion in their decision-making processes. Instead of solely relying on metrics and data—which can lead to missed opportunities and lack of innovation—these board members prioritize the well-being of stakeholders and the greater community, ensuring that their actions align with the organization's purpose and core values. The heart-driven board understands that intuition and emotional intelligence are just as important as logic and data in decision-making.

Such a board recognizes that true leadership requires an integration of the mind and the heart. By embracing their own emotions and encouraging open dialogue, board members create a culture of trust and authenticity within the organization. This fosters a sense of belonging and encourages diverse perspectives, ultimately leading to more innovative and inclusive strategies.

Furthermore, a heart-driven board understands the power of collaboration and collective intelligence. Rather than being driven by ego or personal agendas, these board members actively seek input from all stakeholders, including employees, customers, and community members. By engaging in meaningful dialogue and actively listening to different perspectives, they gain a holistic understanding of complex issues and are better equipped to make informed decisions that benefit the organization and society as a whole.

The heart-driven board also takes into account the long-term impact of its decisions. Instead of focusing solely on short-term gains, it considers the sustainable and ethical implications of its actions. This includes actively pursuing environmental stewardship, promoting social justice, and prioritizing the well-being of future generations.

Revolutionizing governance through a heart-driven board is not without its challenges. It requires a shift in mindset, a commitment to personal growth, and a willingness to challenge traditional norms. However, the potential rewards are immense. By embracing a heart-driven approach, boards can create a positive ripple effect, inspiring other organizations and institutions to adopt a more compassionate and sustainable way of leadership.

Cultivating heart intelligence is a journey that requires self-awareness and a willingness to explore the intertwined nature of intuition and emotional intelligence. It involves directors learning to trust their inner voice, recognize their emotions and those of others, and develop empathy and compassion. By doing so, the heart-driven board can create a culture of trust and collaboration that leads to lasting change.

The Benefits of Heart Intelligence for Board Members

"It is very important to understand that emotional intelligence is not the opposite of intelligence. It is not the triumph of heart over head; it is the unique intersection of both."
— David Caruso

The decisions board members make have a lasting impact on the organizations they serve. They hold the responsibility of setting the direction and strategy of the organization, ensuring its progress towards the defined goals. However, to foster enduring change, a strategic plan alone is insufficient. What is needed is heart intelligence and heart-driven leadership.

Heart intelligence, in the context of decision-making, refers to the capacity to blend intuition and emotional intelligence in order to make choices that align with both personal and organizational values. It enables individuals to access their inner wisdom and establish deeper connections with others, ultimately leading to outcomes that are more meaningful and sustainable.

One of the key benefits of heart intelligence for board members is their enhanced ability to make more informed decisions. By tapping into their intuition, they can access insights that may not be immediately apparent through data analysis alone. Additionally, they can develop a deeper understanding of the emotions and perspectives of those involved in the decision-making process, leading to more holistic and inclusive decision-making.

Another advantage of heart intelligence is the capacity to cultivate stronger relationships with stakeholders. By connecting with others on an emotional level, board members can build trust and foster a sense of community within the organization. This, in turn, can promote greater collaboration, innovation, and ultimately contribute to overall success.

Heart-driven leadership requires a willingness to embrace change and adapt to new situations, something that board members may resist, fearing the unknown. To overcome this barrier, board members should be open to new ideas and be willing to take risks to achieve their goals.

Overcoming Challenges in Developing Heart and Emotional Intelligence

Developing heart and emotional intelligence is a transformative journey that involves overcoming various challenges. While it is a valuable skill to navigate the complexities of emotions and relationships, the path to cultivating heart intelligence is not always easy.

Addressing Skepticism and Doubt

Addressing skepticism and doubt is an important aspect of overcoming challenges in developing heart and emotional intelligence. As individuals embark on the journey of cultivating it, they may encounter skepticism from themselves or others about the relevance and effectiveness of this skill set.

The first step in addressing skepticism is to provide education and raise awareness about the benefits and scientific foundation of heart and emotional intelligence. By understanding the extensive research behind emotional intelligence and its impact on personal and professional success, directors can gain confidence in the value and potential of developing heart intelligence. Sharing information, research findings, success stories, and testimonials can help dispel skepticism and highlight its transformative power.

Encouraging individuals to engage in personal experiences that demonstrate the effectiveness of heart and emotional intelligence can be a persuasive way to address skepticism. When individuals witness firsthand the positive outcomes of emotional intelligence, such as improved relationships, better decision-making, and enhanced well-being, their doubts are likely to diminish. Providing opportunities for directors to practice and apply this type of intelligence skills in real-life situations can help them experience the tangible benefits and overcome skepticism.

Additionally, exposing directors to stories of leaders who have successfully applied emotional intelligence in their personal and professional lives provides concrete evidence of its effectiveness. Role models serve as living examples of how heart and emotional intelligence positively influence relationships, leadership style, and overall success. Learning from their experiences can help individuals see the practical application and value of heart and emotional intelligence.

Building a supportive community of like-minded individuals who are committed to developing heart and emotional intelligence can also dispel skepticism. Engaging in discussions, sharing experiences, and seeking advice from peers who are on a similar journey can help directors overcome doubts and stay motivated. It also creates a safe space to address concerns, share challenges, and celebrate progress, fostering a sense of belonging and a growth mindset.

Developing heart and emotional intelligence is a gradual process that requires patience and persistence. It is important to remind directors that change takes time and setbacks are a natural part of growth. Encouraging perseverance and emphasizing the long-term benefits of emotional intelligence can help them navigate moments of doubt and maintain their commitment to the journey of personal development.

By addressing skepticism head-on and promoting the benefits of heart intelligence, we can create a more emotionally intelligent society, one individual at a time.

Balancing Heart Intelligence With Logic and Reason

While heart intelligence involves tapping into one's emotions, intuition and empathy, it is important to integrate these aspects with rational thinking and logical analysis. This is a key aspect of developing a well-rounded and effective approach to decision-making and problem-solving.

Emotional intelligence plays a crucial role in understanding and managing one's emotions, as well as connecting with others on a deeper level. It allows us to consider the human aspect of decision-making and fosters empathy, compassion, and understanding. Emotions can provide valuable insights and guide us in making choices that align with our values and those of the people we interact with.

While emotions are important, it is equally essential to incorporate rational thinking and logical analysis into the decision-making process. This involves critically evaluating information, examining different perspectives, and considering the practical implications of our choices. Rational thinking helps us assess the risks and benefits, identify potential biases, and make informed decisions based on objective criteria.

Intuition, often associated with heart intelligence, can offer valuable insights that may not be immediately apparent through logical analysis. Integrating intuition with logical thinking allows individuals to make more holistic decisions. When faced with complex or ambiguous situations, listening to their gut feelings can help guide directors in the right direction.

Balancing heart intelligence with logic and reason involves seeking diverse perspectives and engaging in open-minded discussions. By considering a variety of viewpoints, directors can gain a more comprehensive understanding of a situation and make better-informed decisions. Encouraging dialogue and actively listening to different opinions can challenge one's assumptions, expand their thinking, and ensure a more balanced decision-making process.

Developing a balanced approach requires self-reflection and mindfulness. Taking time to pause, reflect, and become aware of their emotions and thoughts allows directors to assess whether their decisions are driven solely by emotions or supported by logical reasoning. Mindfulness practices, such as meditation or journaling, can help cultivate self-awareness and facilitate a more balanced integration of heart intelligence and logic.

Balancing heart intelligence with logic and reason is an ongoing process of learning and growth. It requires a commitment to developing both emotional and intellectual intelligence. Engaging in continuous learning—such as reading books, attending workshops, or seeking feedback—helps expand one's knowledge base and refine their decision-making skills.

By striking a balance between heart intelligence and logic, directors can make well-rounded decisions that consider both the emotional and rational aspects of a situation. Balancing these elements allows them to harness the power of emotions and intuition while grounding their choices in sound reasoning and critical thinking. Achieving this balance enhances their problem-solving abilities, promotes more effective communication, and fosters greater understanding and empathy in their interactions with others. Ultimately, it leads to more successful outcomes and a more harmonious integration of heart and mind.

Embracing Vulnerability and Authenticity

Embracing vulnerability and authenticity is a fundamental aspect of developing heart and emotional intelligence. It involves cultivating the courage to be open, honest, and genuine in our interactions with ourselves and others. By embracing vulnerability, we create a space for deeper connections, empathy, and emotional growth.

Vulnerability is often misunderstood as weakness, but in reality, it is a strength that allows us to show up authentically and genuinely. It involves acknowledging and accepting our own imperfections, fears, and insecurities. When we embrace vulnerability, we create an environment of trust and openness, which enables us to connect with others on a deeper level and build meaningful relationships.

Authenticity is the practice of being true to ourselves, embracing our uniqueness and expressing our thoughts and emotions genuinely. It requires self-awareness and the willingness to show up as our true selves, without pretenses or masks. When we are authentic, we invite others to do the same, fostering an environment where heart intelligence can flourish.

Developing heart intelligence involves being compassionate towards ourselves. It requires acknowledging our own emotions, accepting our vulnerabilities, and treating ourselves with kindness and understanding. Practicing self-compassion allows us to cultivate a strong foundation of self-awareness, self-acceptance, and self-love, which are essential for embracing vulnerability and authenticity.

To foster vulnerability and authenticity, it is important to create safe spaces where individuals feel comfortable sharing their thoughts, emotions, and experiences without fear of judgment or criticism. These spaces can be created through active listening, non-judgmental attitudes, and empathy. When people feel safe to express themselves openly, it encourages the development of heart intelligence in both individuals and groups.

Leaders, especially board directors, play a crucial role in fostering a culture of vulnerability and authenticity. When leaders demonstrate vulnerability, it creates an environment that encourages others to do the same. Sharing personal stories, admitting mistakes, and being open about challenges can inspire trust, empathy, and collaboration among team members. Vulnerable leadership sets the stage for the development of heart intelligence within organizations.

Embracing vulnerability and authenticity is a transformative process that leads to the development of heart intelligence. It requires courage, self-awareness, and a commitment to personal growth. Embracing vulnerability and authenticity not only enhances our own emotional intelligence, but also strengthens our relationships, builds trust, and fosters a more compassionate and empathetic society.

The Role of Technology in Supporting Heart-Driven Leadership

In today's fast-paced and ever-evolving world, technology has become an integral part of people's lives, enabling them to connect, communicate, and work in ways that were once unimaginable. As a board member, it is essential to understand how technology can be leveraged to support heart-driven leadership.

One of the most significant advantages of technology is its ability to facilitate communication and collaboration. With the rise of remote work and virtual teams, technology has made it easier than ever to connect with colleagues and stakeholders from around the world. This has created a more inclusive and diverse workplace, which is essential for cultivating heart intelligence.

Additionally, technology has revolutionized the way data is collected, analyzed, and shared. This is particularly relevant for board members, who are responsible for making strategic decisions based on accurate and reliable information. With the right technology tools, board members can access real-time data, track key performance indicators, and make informed decisions that align with the organization's heart-driven values.

Moreover, technology has also transformed the way individuals learn and develop their skills. With the rise of e-learning, board directors can access training and development programs from anywhere in the world. This is especially important for cultivating heart intelligence, as it allows board members to expand their knowledge and understanding of emotional intelligence, intuition, and other essential leadership skills.

However, it is important to recognize that technology is not a panacea for all organizational challenges. While technology can be a powerful tool for supporting heart-driven leadership, it is essential to balance it with human connection and empathy. At its core, heart intelligence is about developing authentic relationships, fostering trust, and creating a sense of purpose and meaning. While technology can help facilitate these outcomes, it is ultimately up to board members to harness their emotional intelligence and intuition to create lasting change.

The Potential of Heart-Driven Leadership to Create a Better World

"Sometimes the heart sees what
is invisible to the eye."
— Horace Jackson Brown, Jr.

Heart-driven leadership is the practice of leading with the heart. It involves individuals listening to their intuition, connecting with their emotions, and acting from a place of empathy and compassion. This type of leadership is considered essential in creating a better world.

Heart-driven directors understand that leading from the heart means putting people first. They prioritize the well-being of their employees, customers, and stakeholders. They recognize that their decisions impact not just the bottom line, but also the lives of the people they serve.

Heart-driven leadership is also about creating a culture of empathy and compassion. When directors lead with their hearts, they inspire their teams to do the same. They create an environment where people feel valued, supported, and connected.

As board directors, it is essential to cultivate heart intelligence and lead with the heart to create lasting change. By leading with the heart, directors tap into a deeper level of wisdom, empathy, and authenticity that allows them to make decisions aligned with their values and the well-being of all stakeholders.

The potential of a heart-driven board to create a better world is immense. When board members lead with compassion, empathy, and a genuine concern for the well-being of others, they can bring about positive change and transformation at both the organizational and societal levels.

A heart-driven board prioritizes values such as integrity, fairness, and social responsibility in decision-making processes. They go beyond purely financial considerations and take into account the broader impact of their actions on stakeholders, communities, and the environment. They prioritize corporate social responsibility, sustainability, and ethical practices. They understand that success is not solely measured by financial gains, but also by the positive impact they have on people's lives. This mindset encourages innovation, creativity, and a commitment to making a difference in the world.

A heart-driven board also recognizes the importance of collaboration and partnerships. They actively seek opportunities to collaborate with other organizations, nonprofits, and government entities to address complex societal challenges. By leveraging their resources, networks, and expertise, they can tackle issues such as poverty, inequality, environmental sustainability, and social justice on a broader scale.

Furthermore, a heart-driven board sets the tone for the organizational culture. They prioritize employee well-being, inclusivity, and diversity, creating a supportive and empowering work environment. This not only leads to higher employee satisfaction and retention, but also fosters innovation, teamwork, and organizational resilience.

In addition to the internal impact, a heart-driven board can influence the broader business landscape. They can advocate for ethical business practices, transparency, and responsible governance, setting a positive example for other organizations to follow. By actively engaging in public discourse and policy making, they can contribute to shaping a more equitable and sustainable business environment.

Ultimately, the potential of a heart-driven board lies in its ability to inspire and mobilize others. Their actions and decisions demonstrate that it is possible to create successful organizations while also having a positive impact on society. They become role models for other boards, leaders, and aspiring professionals, inspiring them to embrace a heart-driven approach in their own endeavors.

In summary, a heart-driven board has the potential to create a better world by infusing compassion, empathy, and ethical decision-making into the fabric of organizations. Embracing these principles, they foster positive social change, nurture sustainable practices, and inspire others to lead with purpose and integrity. Through their collective efforts, a heart-driven board can contribute to building a more inclusive, equitable, and compassionate society for all.

This book is an invitation to shift our perspective on governance and embrace a more holistic approach that integrates emotional intelligence with strategic thinking. By embracing heart and emotional intelligence, we can forge deeper connections, foster trust, and create an organizational culture that values empathy, compassion, and sustainable outcomes. Let us embrace this opportunity to lead from the heart and together make a positive and transformative impact on the organizations we serve.

SUMMARY OF KEY POINTS

In this book, we have explored the vital role of emotional intelligence in building successful boardroom relationships. Here are some of the key points to take away:

1. **Emotional intelligence is essential for effective governance:** Emotional intelligence is the ability to recognize and manage one's own emotions and those of others. Directors who possess emotional intelligence are more effective communicators, collaborators, and decision-makers.

2. **Emotional intelligence is necessary for building trust:** Trust is paramount in any successful boardroom relationship. Emotional intelligence allows directors to build trust by demonstrating empathy, active listening, and authenticity.

3. **Emotional intelligence enables better conflict management:** Conflict is inevitable in any group setting and boards are no exception. Directors with emotional intelligence are better equipped to manage conflict by remaining calm, objective, and respectful.

4. **Emotional intelligence supports effective decision-making:** The ability to recognize and manage emotions is critical in making sound decisions. Directors with emotional

intelligence are better equipped to weigh the emotional impact of their decisions and consider the perspectives of others.

5. **Emotional   intelligence requires ongoing development:** Emotional intelligence is not a fixed trait but rather a set of skills that can be developed and improved over time. Board directors should prioritize ongoing personal and professional development to enhance their emotional intelligence.

Emotional intelligence is a critical component of effective governance and is essential for building successful boardroom relationships. By recognizing and developing emotional intelligence, board directors can enhance their ability to communicate effectively, build trust, manage conflict, and make sound decisions.

FINAL THOUGHTS ON LEADING WITH EMOTIONAL INTELLIGENCE IN THE BOARDROOM

As some of the most powerful driving forces in today's organizations, all boards should acknowledge the magnitude of the impact they can instill across their enterprises and well beyond. For many years, boards used to place a high priority on a candidate's track record of financial success when selecting new board members. But things have changed. Today, emotional intelligence represents the guiding criterion that dictates the success of organizational boards.

Emotional intelligence can be visualized as a multifaceted lens through which directors perceive, interpret, and react to the emotional dynamics within and outside their organizations. After all, it enables them to navigate complex interpersonal relationships, manage conflicts effectively, and foster an environment of trust and collaboration. From within, emotional intelligence goes well beyond the dynamics confined to the boardroom walls.

This book represents a starting point for each director that wants to contribute toward a better corporate future by shaping their emotional intelligence. As directors, you stand at the helm of your organization, and with that comes a responsibility to lead with wisdom, empathy, and vision. Cultivating emotional intelligence is more than personal growth; it is about setting the tone for your entire organization and shaping a culture that thrives on understanding, resilience, and inclusivity. The greatest leaders are not just those with strategic acumen and industry expertise, but those who can navigate the complex landscape of human interactions with grace and understanding. In today's fast-paced business environment, emotional intelligence is more important than ever.

Throughout this book, we have discussed the role of emotional intelligence in building successful boardroom relationships. We delved into how emotional intelligence can help directors communicate effectively, manage conflict, and build trust with fellow board directors. Furthermore, we have explored how emotional intelligence can enhance decision-making by considering the emotional implications of one's choices.

Moving forward as board director, it is important to continue to develop emotional intelligence skills. This means being open to feedback, seeking out opportunities for growth, and practicing self-reflection. It also means being willing to invest in the emotional well-being of fellow board directors by creating a culture of empathy, respect, and collaboration.

Leading with emotional intelligence in the boardroom is essential for building successful relationships and making strategic decisions that benefit the organization. By continuing to develop their emotional intelligence skills, directors can become more effective and contribute to the long-term success of the organization.

CALL TO ACTION FOR DIRECTORS TO PRIORITIZE EMOTIONAL INTELLIGENCE

In recent years, emotional intelligence has gained significant attention in the business world, and rightfully so. It is among the ten most in-demand skills, as found by the Niagara Institute (2023). Despite its growing importance, research indicates that a mere 20% of leaders perceive themselves as "emotionally intelligent."

Directors' role is to provide strategic direction and oversight of the organization. This means working collaboratively with other directors, as well as with management and various stakeholders. To be effective in this role, directors need to have a high level of emotional intelligence. Having a high EI means being attuned to and in control of one's own emotions and those of others around them. It is a critical skill for building successful relationships, both within and beyond the boardroom.

Here are some reasons why emotional intelligence should be a priority for directors:

It helps build trust: Trust is the foundation of any successful relationship and emotional intelligence is essential for building trust. When directors are emotionally intelligent, they have a greater capacity to understand the needs and concerns of others and to communicate in a way that is authentic and transparent.

It improves decision-making: Boards are responsible for making critical decisions that impact the future of the organization. Emotional intelligence can help directors make better decisions by enabling them to consider the perspectives and emotions of others and by helping directors manage their own emotions in the decision-making process.

It fosters a positive culture: Boards that prioritize emotional intelligence create a culture of respect and collaboration. When directors are emotionally intelligent, they have a greater ability to effectively address and resolve conflicts, work together collaboratively, and create a positive atmosphere for everyone involved.

So, how can directors prioritize emotional intelligence? Here are some tips:

The first step in embracing emotional intelligence is to recognize that it is not a weakness, but rather a strength. Many board members may be hesitant to embrace their intuition and emotions when making decisions, fearing that it will undermine their credibility or appear unprofessional. However, research shows that emotional intelligence can actually enhance one's decision-making abilities and ultimately lead to better outcomes for their organization.

One way to cultivate emotional intelligence is to prioritize self-awareness. Directors should begin by increasing awareness of their own emotions and how those emotions influence their behavior. This involves paying close attention to personal emotional triggers and thought patterns and how they influence their decision-making. By understanding their own biases and tendencies, they can better control them and make more objective decisions.

Another way is to shift the focus from purely logical thinking to a more holistic approach that incorporates both logic and intuition. This means taking the time to listen to one's instincts and inner voice, even if it goes against conventional wisdom or data-driven analysis.

Active listening plays a pivotal role in emotional intelligence. When directors engage in active listening, they convey a sense of appreciation for the opinions and viewpoints of others. This fosters a deeper understanding of their needs and concerns.

Cultivating empathy entails comprehending and sharing the emotions of others. By practicing empathy, directors can foster an environment that is inclusive and supportive for everyone in their vicinity.

Developing critical thinking skills can aid in make better decisions, solving problems more effectively, and becoming a more informed and engaged director. With strong critical thinking skills, directors can assess situations from multiple perspectives, considering both the immediate and long-term implications of their choices. They are better equipped to gather and evaluate relevant data, identify patterns, and make informed judgments based on evidence and logical reasoning.

Considering the multifaceted dynamics uncovered in this book, having a high emotional intelligence skill is essential for successful board directors. It enables them to proficiently manage their own emotions, foster composure, and facilitate rational decision-making, even in high-pressure situations.

Emotional intelligence-driven decision-making takes into account the emotional impact of choices, ensuring fairness and consideration for all stakeholders. Emotional intelligence supports adaptability and resilience—crucial traits for navigating the ever-changing business landscape.

Finally, emotional intelligence enhances stakeholder engagement by addressing emotional needs and maintaining trust and transparency.

Overall, emotional intelligence in the boardroom cultivates strong leadership, effective decision-making, and a supportive environment that contributes to organizational success.

Ethical Governance is a leading firm specializing in providing comprehensive solutions for ethical governance practices. With our deep expertise in board effectiveness and ethical governance, we understand the critical role emotional intelligence plays in the boardroom.

Our firm specializes in emotional intelligence training specifically tailored for board directors. Our team of experienced consultants works closely with boards to provide actionable insights and recommendations for enhancing emotional intelligence within the boardroom. By partnering with Ethical Governance, boards can foster a culture of emotional intelligence, leading to improved ethical decision-making, stronger leadership, and enhanced board dynamics.

We invite you to reach out to us to explore how we can support you in enhancing director effectiveness and driving improved organizational performance.

Contact us through this link:
https://ethicalgovernance.com.au/contact-us

or via email at:
info@ethicalgovernance.com.au

REFERENCES

Adams, R. B., Hermalin, B. E., & Weisbach, M. S., 2010. The role of boards of directors in corporate governance: A conceptual framework and survey. *Journal of Economic Literature,* 48(1), 58-107.

Ashkanasy, N. M., & Daus, C. S., 2002. Emotion in the workplace: The new challenge for managers. *Academy of Management Perspectives*, 16(1), 76-86.

Ashkanasy, N.M. and Daus, C.S., 2005. Rumors of the death of emotional intelligence in organizational behavior are vastly exaggerated. *Journal of Organizational Behavior*, 26(4), pp.441-452.

Association for Talent Development, 2019 'Succession Planning: Is Your Organization Prepared?', *Association for Talent Development*. Available at: https://www.td.org/insights/succession-planning-is-your-organization-prepared

Barsade, S. G., 2002. The ripple effect: Emotional contagion and its influence on group behavior. *Administrative Science Quarterly*, 47(4), 644-675.

Bechara, A., Damasio, H., Damasio, A. R., & Lee, G. P., 1999. Different contributions of the human amygdala and ventromedial prefrontal cortex to decision-making. *Journal of Neuroscience*, 19(13), 5473-5481.

Bechara, A., Damasio, H., Tranel, D. and Damasio, A.R., 1997. Deciding advantageously before knowing the advantageous strategy. *Science*, 275(5304), pp.1293-1295.

Boyatzis, R. E., Rochford, K., & Taylor, S. N., 2015. The role of the positive emotional attractor in vision and shared vision: Toward effective leadership, relationships, and engagement. *Frontiers in Psychology*, 6, 670.

Boyatzis, R., & McKee, A., 2005. Resonant leadership: Renewing yourself and connecting with others through mindfulness, hope, and compassion. *Harvard Business Press*.

Boyatzis, R.E., 2008. Competencies in the 21st century. *Journal of Management Development*, 27(1), pp.5-12.

Boyatzis, R.E., Goleman, D. and Rhee, K., 2000. Clustering competence in emotional intelligence: Insights from the Emotional Competence Inventory (ECI). *Handbook of Emotional Intelligence*, 99(6), pp.343-362.

Boyatzis, R.E., Smith, M.L. and Blaize, N., 2006. Developing sustainable leaders through coaching and compassion. *Academy of Management Learning & Education*, 5(1), pp.8-24.

Brackett, M. A., & Mayer, J. D., 2003. Convergent, discriminant, and incremental validity of competing measures of emotional intelligence. *Personality and Social Psychology Bulletin*, 29(9), 1147-1158.

Brackett, M.A., Rivers, S.E. and Salovey, P., 2011. Emotional intelligence: Implications for personal, social, academic, and workplace success. *Social and Personality Psychology Compass*, 5(1), pp.88-103.

Cameron, K.S. and Caza, A., 2004. Introduction: Contributions to the discipline of positive organizational scholarship. *American Behavioral Scientist*, 47(6), pp.731-739.

Cannon, W. B., 1927. The James-Lange theory of emotions: A critical examination and an alternative theory. *The American Journal of Psychology*, 39(1/4), 106-124.

CareerBuilder, 2011. 'More Than Two-Thirds of Workers Said Their Manager Sets a Good Example in the Workplace, According to New CareerBuilder.ca Survey', *CareerBuilder*. Available at: https://www.careerbuilder.ca/share/aboutus/pressreleasesdetail.aspx?id =pr652&sd=8%2f18%2f2011&ed=8%2f18%2f2099

Carter, D. A., Simkins, B. J., & Simpson, W. G., 2003. Corporate governance, board diversity, and firm value. *Financial Review*, 38(1), 33-53.

Catalyst, 2020. 'Empathy at Work: A Strategy for Crisis', *Catalyst*. Available at: https://www.catalyst.org/reports/empathy-work-strategy-crisis/

Caza, A. and Cameron, K.S., 2008. Positive organizational scholarship: What does it achieve. *Handbook of Macro-organizational Behavior*, pp.99-116.

CEDR, 2019. 'Conflicts in the Boardroom: Survey Results and Analysis', *Centre for Effective Dispute Resolution*. Available at: https://www.cedr.com/wp-content/uploads/2019/10/Conflicts_in_the_Boardroom_Survey_Result s_and_Analysis.pdf

Chen, G. M., & Starosta, W. J., 2000. The development and validation of the intercultural communication sensitivity scale. *Human Communication*, 3(1), 1-15.

Cherniss, C. & Adler, M., 2000. Promoting emotional intelligence in organizations: Make training in emotional intelligence effective. *American Society for Training and Development*.

Ciarrochi, J., Deane, F.P. and Anderson, S., 2002. Emotional intelligence moderates the relationship between stress and mental health. *Personality and Individual Differences, 32*(2), pp.197-209.

Cooper, R.K., 1997. 'Applying emotional intelligence in the workplace', Training and Development, 51(12), 31+, available: https://link.gale.com/apps/doc/A20251750/AONE?u=anon~eefaf7c9&sid=googleScholar&xid=106ba75c

Côté, S. and Miners, C.T., 2006. Emotional intelligence, cognitive intelligence, and job performance. *Administrative Science Quarterly, 51*(1), pp.1-28.

Coutu, D.L., 2002. How resilience works. *Harvard Business Review, 80*(5), pp.46-56.

Craig, A. D., 2009. How do you feel—now? The anterior insula and human awareness. *Nature Reviews Neuroscience*, 10(1), 59-70.

Damasio, A.R., 1994. Descartes' error and the future of human life. *Scientific American, 271*(4), pp.144-144.

Day, D.V., Fleenor, J.W., Atwater, L.E., Sturm, R.E. & McKee, R.A., 2014. Advances in leader and leadership development: A review of 25 years of research and theory. *The Leadership Quarterly, 25*(1), pp.63-82.

Day, D.V., Harrison, M.M. and Halpin, S.M., 2008. An integrative approach to leader development: Connecting adult development, identity, and expertise. *Routledge.*

Deloitte, 2020. 'The ABCs of Boardroom Dynamics', *Deloitte.* Available at: https://www2.deloitte.com/content/dam/Deloitte/in/Documents/risk/Board%20of%20Directors/in-gc-the-abcs-of-boardroom-dynamicsnoexp.pdf

Deloitte, 2023. 'Business leaders recognize importance of trust but do not prioritize', *Deloitte*. Available at: https://www.deloitte.com/global/en/about/press-room/business-leaders-recognize-importance-of-trust-but-do-not-prioritize.html

Dijksterhuis, A., Bos, M.W., Nordgren, L.F. and Van Baaren, R.B., 2006. On making the right choice: The deliberation-without-attention effect. *Science*, *311*(5763), pp.1005-1007.

Diligent, 2019 'What is a Board Succession Planning Policy?', *Diligent Insights*. Available at: https://www.diligent.com/insights/board-succession-planning/what-is-a-board-succession-planning-policy/

Druskat, V. U., & Wolff, S. B., 2001. Building the emotional intelligence of groups. *Harvard Business Review*, 79(3), 80-90.

Druskat, V.U. and Wolff, S.B., 2001. Group emotional intelligence and its influence on group effectiveness. *The emotionally intelligent workplace: How to select for, measure, and improve emotional intelligence in individuals, groups and organizations*, pp.132-155.

Dulewicz, V. and Herbert, P., 2004. Does the composition and practice of boards of directors bear any relationship to the performance of their companies?. *Corporate Governance: An International Review*, *12*(3), pp.263-280.

Eccles, R. G., Newquist, S. C., & Schatz, R., 2007. Reputation and Its Risks, *Harvard Business Review*, February 2007. Available at: https://hbr.org/2007/02/reputation-and-its-risks

Edmondson, A. C., 1999. Psychological safety and learning behavior in work teams. *Administrative Science Quarterly*, 44(2), 350-383.

Ekman, P. and Friesen, W.V., 2003. Unmasking the face: A guide to recognizing emotions from facial clues (Vol. 10).

Ekman, P., 1999. Basic emotions. In T. Dalgleish & M. Power (Eds.), Handbook of Cognition and Emotion (pp. 45-60). *John Wiley & Sons.*

Elfenbein, H.A., Druskat, V.U., Sala, F. and Mount, G., 2006. Team emotional intelligence: What it can mean and how it can affect performance. *Linking emotional intelligence and performance at work: Current research evidence with individuals and groups*, pp.165-184.

Ely, R. J., & Thomas, D. A., 2001. Cultural diversity at work: The effects of diversity perspectives on work group processes and outcomes. *Administrative Science Quarterly*, 46(2), 229-273.

Emmons, R.A., McCullough, M.E. and Tsang, J.A., 2003. The assessment of gratitude.

Equilar, 2017. 'Hundreds of Companies Disclose Board Skills Matrices', *Equilar Blog*. Available at: https://www.equilar.com/blogs/241-hundreds-of-companies-disclose-board-skills-matrices.html.

Erhardt, N. L., Werbel, J. D., & Shrader, C. B., 2003. Board of director diversity and firm financial performance. *Corporate Governance: An International Review*, 11(2), 102-111.

Ernst and Young, 2020. 'The Hive: Ethical Boardroom Decision-Making', *Raconteur*. Available at: https://insights.raconteur.net/the-hive-ethical-boardroom-decision-making

Eurich, T., 2017. Insight: The power of self-awareness in a self-deluded world. *Macmillan.*

Eurich, T., 2018. 'Working with People Who Aren't Self-Aware',

Harvard Business Review, October 3. Available at: https://hbr.org/2018/10/working-with-people-who-arent-self-aware

Feruglio, S., Panasiti, M.S., Crescentini, C., Aglioti, S.M. and Ponsi, G., 2022. The impact of mindfulness meditation on social and moral behavior: Does mindfulness enhance other-oriented motivation or decrease monetary reward salience? *Frontiers in Integrative Neuroscience, 16.*

Fombrun, C.J., Gardberg, N.A. and Sever, J.M., 2000. The Reputation Quotient SM: A multi-stakeholder measure of corporate reputation. *Journal of Brand Management, 7,* pp.241-255.

Fredrickson, B. L., 2001. The role of positive emotions in positive psychology: The broaden-and-build theory of positive emotions. *The American Psychologist,* 56(3), 218-226.

Freeman, R. E., Harrison, J. S., & Wicks, A. C., 2007. Managing for Stakeholders: Survival, Reputation, and Success. *Yale University Press.*

French, R. and Simpson, P., 2018. Attention, cooperation, purpose: An approach to working in groups using insights from Wilfred Bion. *Routledge.*

Galinsky, A. D., Maddux, W. W., Gilin, D., & White, J. B., 2008. Why it pays to get inside the head of your opponent: The differential effects of perspective taking and empathy in negotiations. *Psychological Science,* 19(4), 378-384.

Galinsky, A.D. and Ku, G., 2004. The effects of perspective-taking on prejudice: The moderating role of self-evaluation. *Personality and Social Psychology Bulletin, 30*(5), pp.594-604.

Gigerenzer, G. and Gaissmaier, W., 2011. Heuristic decision making.

Annual Review of Psychology, 62, pp.451-482.

Gitnux, 2023. 'Reputation Management Statistics', *Gitnux Blog*. Available at: https://blog.gitnux.com/reputation-management-statistics/.

Goleman, D. 2015. 'How Emotional Intelligence Became a Key Leadership Skill', *Harvard Business Review*. Available at: https://hbr.org/2015/04/how-emotional-intelligence-became-a-key-leadership-skill.

Goleman, D. and Cherniss, C., 2001., The emotionally intelligent workplace: How to select for, measure, and improve emotional intelligence in individuals, groups, and organizations (pp. 121-128) San Francisco, CA: *Jossey-Bass*.

Goleman, D., 1995. Emotional intelligence: Why it can matter more than IQ. *Bantam Books*.

Goleman, D., 1998. Working with emotional intelligence. *Bantam Books*.

Goleman, D., Boyatzis, R. E., & McKee, A., 2013. Primal leadership: Unleashing the power of emotional intelligence. *Harvard Business Review Press*.

Gottman, J.M. and Levenson, R.W., 1992. Marital processes predictive of later dissolution: behavior, physiology, and health. *Journal of Personality and Social Psychology, 63*(2), p.221.

Grandey, A. A., 2000. Emotion regulation in the workplace: A new way to conceptualize emotional labor. *Journal of Occupational Health Psychology*, 5(1), 95-110.

Grant, A.M. and Gino, F., 2010. A little thanks goes a long way: Explaining why gratitude expressions motivate prosocial behavior. *Journal of Personality and Social Psychology, 98*(6), p.946.

Griffin, T., Larcker, D.F., Miles, S. and Tayan, B., 2017. Board evaluations and boardroom dynamics. Rock Center for Corporate Governance at Stanford University Closer Look Series: Topics, Issues and Controversies in Corporate Governance No. CGRP63, *Stanford University Graduate School of Business Research Paper*, (17-22).

Gross, J. J., 2015. Emotion regulation: Current status and future prospects. *Psychological Inquiry*, 26(1), 1-26.

Hafenbrack, A.C., Kinias, Z. and Barsade, S.G., 2014. Debiasing the mind through meditation: Mindfulness and the sunk-cost bias. *Psychological Science*, 25(2), pp.369-376.

Hannah, S.T., Avolio, B.J., Luthans, F. and Harms, P.D., 2008. Leadership efficacy: Review and future directions. *The Leadership Quarterly*, 19(6), pp.669-692.

Hitt, M. A., Ireland, R. D., & Hoskisson, R. E., 2019. Strategic management: concepts and cases: competitiveness and globalization. *Cengage Learning*.

Hochschild, A. R., 1983. The managed heart: Commercialization of human feeling. *University of California Press*.

Hofmann, W., Luhmann, M., Fisher, R. R., Vohs, K. D., & Baumeister, R. F., 2012. Yes, but are they happy? Effects of trait self-control on affective well-being and life satisfaction. *Journal of Personality*, 80(2), 33

Hofstede, G., 1997. Cultures and Organizations. Software of the Mind. New York: McGraw-Hill.

Homan, A.C., Hollenbeck, J.R., Humphrey, S.E., Knippenberg, D.V., Ilgen, D.R. and Van Kleef, G.A., 2008. Facing differences with an open mind: Openness to experience, salience of intragroup differences, and performance of diverse work groups. *Academy of Management Journal*, *51*(6), pp.1204-1222.

Hsee, C. K., & Hastie, R., 2006. Decision and experience: Why don't we choose what makes us happy? *Trends in Cognitive Sciences*, 10(1), 31-37.

Hülsheger, U. R., Alberts, H. J., Feinholdt, A., & Lang, J. W., 2013. Benefits of mindfulness at work: The role of mindfulness in emotion regulation, emotional exhaustion, and job satisfaction. *Journal of Applied Psychology*, 98(2), 310-325.

Huse, M., 2005. Accountability and creating accountability: A framework for exploring behavioural perspectives of corporate governance. *British Journal of Management*, 16(S1), S65-S79.

Huse, M., 2007. Boards, governance, and value creation: The human side of corporate governance. *Cambridge University Press*.

James, W., 1884. What is an emotion? *Mind*, 9(34), 188-205.

Jones, D. A., Willness, C. R., & Glavas, A., 2014. When Corporate Social Responsibility (CSR) Meets Organizational Psychology: New Frontiers in Micro-CSR Research, Ethics, and Organizational Behavior. *Journal of Organizational Behavior*, 35(3), 428-441.

Jordan, P. J., & Troth, A. C., 2004. Managing emotions during team problem solving: Emotional intelligence and conflict resolution. *Human Performance*, 17(2), 195-218.

Joseph, D.L. and Newman, D.A., 2010. Emotional intelligence: an integrative meta-analysis and cascading model. *Journal of Applied Psychology*, 95(1), p.54.

Kahneman, D. and Tversky, A., 2013. Prospect theory: An analysis of decision under risk. In *Handbook of the fundamentals of financial decision making: Part I* (pp. 99-127).

Kahneman, D., 2011. Thinking, fast and slow. *Macmillan*.

Kiel, G. C., & Nicholson, G. J., 2003. Board composition and corporate performance: How the Australian experience informs contrasting theories of corporate governance. *Corporate Governance: An International Review*, 11(3), 189-205.

Kluger, A.N. and DeNisi, A., 1996. The effects of feedback interventions on performance: a historical review, a meta-analysis, and a preliminary feedback intervention theory. *Psychological Bulletin*, *119*(2), p.254.

Korn Ferry, n.d. 'Director's Toolbox: Emotional Intelligence', *Korn Ferry*. Available at: https://www.kornferry.com/insights/this-week-in-leadership/directors-toolbox-emotional-intelligence.

Kring, A. M., & Sloan, D. M., 2009. Emotion regulation and psychopathology: A transdiagnostic approach to etiology and treatment. *Guilford Press*.

Kunda, Z., 1990. The case for motivated reasoning. *Psychological Bulletin*, 108(3), 480-498.

Lazarus, R. S., 1991. Emotion and adaptation. *Oxford University Press*.

LeDoux, J. E., 2000. Emotion circuits in the brain. *Annual Review of Neuroscience*, 23(1), 155-184.

Lerner, J. S., & Keltner, D., 2000. Beyond valence: Toward a model of emotion-specific influences on judgment and choice. *Cognition and Emotion*, 14(4), 473-493.

Lerner, J. S., Li, Y., Valdesolo, P., & Kassam, K. S., 2015. Emotion and decision making. *Annual Review of Psychology*, 66, 799-823.

Levenson, R. W., 1999. The intrapersonal functions of emotion. Cognition and Emotion, 13(5), 481-504.

Locke, E.A. and Latham, G.P., 2002. Building a practically useful theory of goal setting and task motivation: A 35-year odyssey. *American Psychologist, 57*(9), p.705.

Loewenstein, G. F., Weber, E. U., Hsee, C. K., & Welch, N., 2001. Risk as feelings. *Psychological Bulletin*, 127(2), 267-28.

Mahanta, M., Goswami, K., 2020. Exploring the role of ethics in the emotional intelligence-organizational commitment relationship. *Asian Journal of Business Ethics* 9, 275–303.

Matsumoto, D., 2006. Are Cultural Differences in Emotion Regulation Mediated by Personality Traits? *Journal of Cross-Cultural Psychology, 37*(4), 421–437.

Mayer, J.D., Caruso, D.R. and Salovey, P., 1997. *Emotional Intelligence Meets.*

McCraty, R. and Childre, D., 2010. Coherence: bridging personal, social, and global health. *Altern Ther Health Med, 16*(4), pp.10-24.

McCraty, R., Atkinson, M., Tomasino, D., Bradley, R., 2009. The Coherent Heart Heart–Brain Interactions, Psychophysiological Coherence, and the Emergence of System-Wide Order. *Integral Review*. 5.

McKinsey, 2017. 'Successfully transitioning to new leadership roles', *McKinsey & Company*. Available at: https://www.mckinsey.com/capabilities/people-and-organizational-performance/our-insights/successfully-transitioning-to-new-leadership-roles.

Mesquita, B., & Albert, D., 2007. The cultural regulation of emotions. In J. J. Gross (Ed.), *Handbook of Emotion Regulation* (pp. 486-503). Guilford Press.

Miloff, M., 2017. JCamp 180 (n.d.) 'Board Recruitment Toolkit', JCamp 180, *Knowledge Center*. Available at: https://jcamp180.org/JCamp180/media/Media/Knowledge-Center/Governance/BoardRecruitmentToolkit.pdf.

Moore, D.A., Loewenstein, G., Tanlu, L. and Bazerman, M.H., 2003. Auditor independence, conflict of interest, and the unconscious intrusion of bias. *Division of Research, Harvard Business School.*

Murphy, K.J., 2013. Executive compensation: Where we are, and how we got there. In *Handbook of the Economics of Finance* (Vol. 2, pp. 211-356). Elsevier.

Narayan, A., 2020. 'Three Dimensions of Corporate Reputation', LinkedIn. Available at: https://www.linkedin.com/pulse/three-dimensions-corporate-reputation-amit-narayan/.

Neale, M. A., Huber, V. L., & Northcraft, G. B., 1987. The framing of negotiations: Contextual influences on negotiation outcomes. *Research in Organizational Behavior*, 9, 163-225.

Niagara Institute, 2023. 'Emotional Intelligence Statistics', *Niagara Institute Blog*. Available at: https://www.niagarainstitute.com/blog/emotional-intelligence-statistics.

Nielsen, K., Nielsen, M.B., Ogbonnaya, C., Känsälä, M., Saari, E. and Isaksson, K., 2017. Workplace resources to improve both employee well-being and performance: A systematic review and meta-analysis.

Work & Stress, 31(2), pp.101-120.

O'Boyle Jr, E.H., Humphrey, R.H., Pollack, J.M., Hawver, T.H. and Story, P.A., 2011. The relation between emotional intelligence and job performance: A meta-analysis. *Journal of Organizational Behavior, 32*(5), pp.788-818.

Ochsner, K. N., & Gross, J. J., 2005. The cognitive control of emotion. *Trends in Cognitive Sciences, 9*(5), 242-249.

OnBoard Meetings, 2022. 'Board Skills Matrix: An Essential Tool', *OnBoard Meetings Blog*. Available at: https://www.onboardmeetings.com/blog/board-skills-matrix-essential-tool/.

Page, S.E., 2007. Making the difference: Applying a logic of diversity. *Academy of Management Perspectives, 21*(4), pp.6-20.

Pairin, n.d. 'Soft Skills: The Primary Predictor of Success in Academics, Career and Life', Pairin. Available at: https://www.pairin.com/soft-skills-primary-predictor-success-academics-career-life/.

Pink, D.H., 2011. Drive: The surprising truth about what motivates us. *Penguin.*

Porges, S.W., 2011. The polyvagal theory: Neurophysiological foundations of emotions, attachment, communication, and self-regulation (Norton Series on Interpersonal Neurobiology*). WW Norton & Company.*

PricewaterhouseCoopers (PwC), 2022. 'Annual Corporate Directors Survey', *PwC Governance Insights Center*. Available at: https://www.pwc.com/us/en/services/governance-insights-center/library/annual-corporate-directors-survey.html.

Rae, S., 2018. Moral choices: An introduction to ethics. *Zondervan Academic*.

Rathod, L., 2018. 'Effective Boards and Maintaining Healthy Boardroom Dynamics', *Diligent*. Available at: https://www.diligent.com/en-gb/blog/effective-boards-and-maintaining-healthy-boardroom-dynamics-diligent/.

Reynolds, P., 2022. 'Strategic Leadership: How to Think, Act and Influence Others More Strategically', *Harvard Division of Continuing Education*. Available at: https://professional.dce.harvard.edu/blog/strategic-leadership/.

Salovey, P., & Mayer, J. D., 1990. Emotional intelligence. Imagination, Cognition and Personality, 9(3), 185-211.

Salovey, P., Mayer, J.D., Caruso, D. and Yoo, S.H., 2009. The positive psychology of emotional intelligence.

Shalett, L., 2020. 'The Business Case for Trust: How Trusting Your Employees Can Improve Your Bottom Line', *People + Strategy*, Summer 2020. Available at: https://www.shrm.org/executive/resources/people-strategy-journal/summer2020/Pages/feature-shalett.aspx.

Shapiro, J., 2020. 'ASX boards remain invitation-only, says Ownership Matters study', *Australian Financial Review*. Available at: https://www.afr.com/markets/equity-markets/asx-boards-remain-invitation-only-says-ownership-matters-study-20201023-p56806.

Sharot, T., Korn, C. W., & Dolan, R. J., 2011. How unrealistic optimism is maintained in the face of reality. *Nature Neuroscience*, 14(11), 1475-1479.

Smither, J.W., London, M. and Reilly, R.R., 2005. Does performance improve following multisource feedback? A theoretical model, meta-analysis, and review of empirical findings. *Personnel Psychology*, *58*(1), pp.33-66.

Solomon, J., & Solomon, A., 2020. Corporate governance and accountability. John Wiley & Sons.

Sonnenfeld, J.A., 2002. What makes great boards great. *Harvard Business Review*, *80*(9), pp.106-113.

Sosik, J. J., & Megerian, L. E., 2011. Understanding leader emotional intelligence and performance: The role of self-other agreement on transformational leadership perceptions. *Group and Organization Management*, 36(6), 719-747.

Strack, F., Martin, L. L., & Stepper, S., 1988. Inhibiting and facilitating conditions of the human smile: A nonobtrusive test of the facial feedback hypothesis. *Journal of Personality and Social Psychology*, 54(5), 768-777.

Strategy - Business, 2015, 'The Leadership Journey', *Strategy - Business*. Available at: https://www.strategy-business.com/article/00327.

Sundaramurthy, C. and Lewis, M.W., 2003. Paradoxes of governance: managing control and collaboration. *Academy of Management Review*, *28*(3), pp.397-415.

Szczygiel, D.D. and Mikolajczak, M., 2018. Emotional intelligence buffers the effects of negative emotions on job burnout in nursing. *Frontiers in Psychology*, *9*, p.2649.

Tannenbaum, S.I., Mathieu, J.E., Salas, E. and Cannon-Bowers, J.A., 1991. Meeting trainees' expectations: The influence of training fulfillment on the development of commitment, self-efficacy, and motivation. *Journal of Applied Psychology*, *76*(6), p.759.

Tooby, J. and Cosmides, L., 2008. The evolutionary psychology of the emotions and their relationship to internal regulatory variables.

Treviño, L.K., Butterfield, K.D. and McCabe, D.L., 1998. The ethical context in organizations: Influences on employee attitudes and behaviors. *Business Ethics Quarterly*, 8(3), pp.447-476.

Tricker, R. I., 2015. Corporate governance: Principles, policies, and practices. Oxford University Press.

Uhl-Bien, M., 2006. Relational leadership theory: Exploring the social processes of leadership and organizing. *The Leadership Quarterly*, *17*(6), pp.654-676.

UNECE, 2022. Branding and reputation management are key to safeguarding trust in official statistics – new UNECE guidelines show how, *United Nations Economic Commission for Europe*. Available at: https://unece.org/media/Statistics/news/370220.

Van Kleef, G.A., De Dreu, C.K. and Manstead, A.S., 2010. An interpersonal approach to emotion in social decision making: The emotions as social information model. In *Advances in Experimental Social Psychology* (Vol. 42, pp. 45-96). Academic Press.

Vantage Circle (n.d.) 'Emotional Intelligence in the Workplace', *Vantage Circle Blog*. Available at: https://blog.vantagecircle.com/emotional-intelligence-in-the-workplace/.

Watermark Search International, 2023. 'Board Diversity Index', *Watermark Search*. Available at: https://www.watermarksearch.com.au/thought-leadership/2023-board-diversity-index.

Weber, L., 2010. Goodreads. Available at: https://www.goodreads.com/author/show/884684.Liz_Weber

Women Serve on Boards, 2022. 'How Board Directors Can Develop Crucial Emotional Intelligence', *Women Serve on Boards*. Available at: https://www.womenserveonboards.com/2022/02/25/how-board-directors-can-develop-crucial-emotional-intelligence/.

Zhu, W., May, D.R. and Avolio, B.J., 2004. The impact of ethical leadership behavior on employee outcomes: The roles of psychological empowerment and authenticity. *Journal of Leadership & Organizational Studies*, *11*(1), pp.16-26.

www.ingramcontent.com/pod-product-compliance
Lightning Source LLC
Chambersburg PA
CBHW040753220326
41597CB00029BA/4757